Pivot

Real Cut-Through Stories By Experts At The Frontline Of Agility and Transformation

Agility Gigs Community

WRITING MATTERS PUBLISHING

Pivot: Real, Cut-Through Stories By Experts At The Frontline Of Agility and Transformation

First published in October 2018

Writing Matters Publishing (UK)
info@writingmatterspublishing.com
www.writingmatterspublishing.com

ISBN 978-1-912774-03-6 (Pbk)

Editors: Matt Bradley, Adrian Stalham and Andrew Priestley

Contributors: Adrian Stalham, Jacqueline Shakespeare, Scott Potter, Brett Ansley, Wayne Palmer, Matt Bradley, Bhavesh Vaghela, Angie Main, Karan Jain, Andrew Kidd, David Smith, Ahmed Syed, John Coleman, Mike Nuttall, Bruce Thompson, Jessica Gilbert, John Boyes.

Contents

Foreword

Agile is dead but agility is alive and well.

But now what was the exclusive methodology of technology teams has been reborn as a business philosophy underpinned by all manner of transformation. That is the essence of agility and to attain it requires a great deal of leadership tenacity.

In fact, think about any form of change in which you have been involved with and the highs and lows associated with it. What if you had firsthand insight into the things that could go wrong or indeed numerous examples of great transformation in order to help you deliver successful outcomes.

However, the life of a Change Agent, Manager or Leader can be lonely because the associated risks of something going wrong are high. Indeed, I have personally been quoted a number of times saying that I almost got fired by introducing new things into the places where I have worked. Be that new technology, products, services or even ways of working.

To that end, in my humble opinion, the best transformation comes via cultural transformation. And oh, how I wish I knew that many years ago. But all too often we are afraid to tackle workplace toxicity, delve into the world of emotions nor have a playbook for aligning mindsets.

Many of us have these insights from our experiences and we tend to share our battle scars through storytelling, albeit to a small circle of colleagues or the occasional public presentations. Thankfully, this book represents a treasure trove of relevant stories, from the world of agile transformation, shared generously by those who have real-world experience and a passion for transformation.

Let me tell you that failing fast is no longer option in business anymore, although some may say that it never was, and hence today's world calls for pivoting quickly. So why not tap into the knowledge of others and minimise your battle scars.

Therefore, no matter what role you have in your organisation, this book will help to steer you away from the rocks of failure and drive you towards the success of great transformation.

Fin Goulding, *International CIO* at Aviva

Co-Author of *Flow: A Handbook for Change-Makers, Mavericks, Innovation Activists & Leaders* and *12 Steps to Flow: The New Framework for Business Agility.*

Welcome

"Blessed are the Weird People - the poets, misfits, writers, mystics, heretics, painters and troubadours - for they teach us to see the world through different eyes." - Jacob Nordby

Organisations have never been under so much pressure to change.

For many, over the past few years, Agile has been the great hope. Implement Agile and your problems will be fixed. Use this framework, send all your teams on a two day training course and hey presto!

The reality has been very different.

This book does promote the use of Agile, but not in a prescriptive sense. It is about appreciating the Agile values and understanding the need for experimentation. The need to reflect and adjust course. The understanding that most things are not knowable in advance, they need to emerge. If you have an approach that can't deal with emerging insight, an approach that has rigid plans based on big, upfront design, this book will help you realise that you need a different, more flexible approach. This is the reality of transformation.

What follows are short stories by experts who have been on the front line of helping organisations and people change. They talk about real problems, and the way they solved them. You won't find these stories in the glorified case studies, or guides, or frameworks.

The authors are all part of *Sullivan & Stanley's Agility Gigs* community. A collective of CxO's, Coaches, Change Agents and Product Specialists. The community acts as a supportive think-tank and knowledge sharing environment, where members talk openly about challenges, while gathering feedback and insights from other others in the industry. The key is trust and relationships.

Through both an online experience (via a social network) and offline experience (via workshops and meet ups) the group has explored organisational design, scaling, releasing agility, systems thinking and what it means to have an agile mindset.

This book was born out of one of these sessions.

Best-selling author and publisher Andrew Priestley ran a session on sharing your IP, and the idea to co-create a book was an obvious outcome.

We invited the authors to write their stories under one of the four agile values from *The Agile Manifesto*. Interestingly, the authors focused on three of the four values only, with the majority went with individuals and interactions over processes and tools.

Perhaps we shouldn't be surprised by that, in the end it always comes down to being about people.

Enjoy!

Matt Bradley and Adrian Stalham

Sullivan & Stanley

Individuals and Interactions
Over Processes and Tools

"Leaders and Cultures and Heretics, Oh My !"
Dorothy in *The Wizard of Oz* (paraphrased)

Adrian Stalham

All transformations are about people. End of.

Change management is an oxymoron. It can be guided and nudged at best. Trust us humans to suggest we can put a flawed organisational construct (management) over the change of behaviours needed in people.

Ah, the arrogance of bureaucracy.

Agile values and principles teach us common sense. To sense and adapt. To allow things to emerge in a complex adaptive system. To reflect and improve. Lots of sensible things that, for some reason, we struggle to make common practice.

I have been involved in many organisational transformations, across many industries, involving many different teams in many departments and many commercial initiatives. Many of them have been Agile related. The details are irrelevant. If you want to be good in this game, you need to understand people. Not just as in 'I'm a person, of course I understand people'. I mean truly understand people. In my early days as a project manager, my favourite sweeping statement (when asked about the skills needed for the role) was 'you need to be a psychologist first'. I have other sweeping statements. I will no doubt share them later.

My interest in how people think and behave was therefore born early in my career. I have always been fascinated in why we do certain things, in certain situations. How our supposedly independent minds can become quite predictable (all together now – 'we are all individuals').

What causes our unpredictability in other situations? Our cognitive biases and how they alter our perception of facts. How we game things even though we know it's not right.

My story is about people. About how change happens. About how it can't be predicted and instead needs to be cultivated. Like a small plant. We don't manage a seedling by putting under the management of a more senior plant who directs it in the actions and processes of a growing plant. Instead, we manage the environment around it. The sunlight, the nutrients, the water, the temperature. We monitor and adjust. A bit more of this, less of that – oops better try some of this instead. If we get that right, we get growth. Same with people.

The context of my story is a Financial Services organisation.

The team were working on a 50 year old product with closely coupled architecture and lots of manual testing. It was a proud, close knit team – but they were simply using outdated working practices. The product was high quality with envious performance levels, but the world around them had changed and simply being good was no longer enough. My role was to introduce agile/lean ways of working, CI/CD and automated testing.

Pivot 1 – Leadership moments vs Humanistic needs

"A leader is best when people barely know they exist,
when the leader's work is done, their aim fulfilled, the people will say:
we did it ourselves." Lao Tzu (adjusted for inclusivity)

The team's Delivery Manager was ambitious. We'll call him Nik (after all, it's his name). He had recently landed and could see the need to help the team improve. Nik had been part of an agile team before and he knew what good looked like. He's the kind of guy who leads from the front. Wears his heart on his sleeve. An extrovert and highly driven. I think Nik would now agree that in those early days, his *Emotional Intelligence* was running on low.

I was the Transformation Lead assigned to this particular product. We were shifting from projects to products and had an ambition to tackle automation, tooling and coaching. The transformation also delved into the Product, Finance and Infrastructure teams. It's never just about IT. I met Nik one summer's day and he was glad we had arrived. He had been trying to get the change going alone, with limited success so far.

Nik's natural preference to lead had generated a town hall explanation of the direction (a move to scrum), why (it's better), how it would happen (you can self-organise yourselves) and a timeline (it starts next week). Nik had put a stake in the ground, sounded the bugle of rationality, mounted his white charger and cried *Follow me!* Trouble is, when he looked over his shoulder, no-one was following. So, Nik organised the new team constructs himself (as the team seemed unwilling to do it) but announced they could move their desks to sit in their new teams. A week later and no-one had moved. Nik helped that process happen too.

Nik's heart was absolutely in the right place.

He considered it a leadership moment and he acted in that way. The team however, were not happy. The team were close knit and proud. Many were unwilling to speak up in big groups, especially with their leader present. It was the quietest, and strongest, revolution I had seen.

Early in the engagement, my team coaching sessions were actually quite well attended. Lots of questions and engagement. But it was obvious I needed to get them in small groups, or alone, to get the full story.

The team were actually willing to learn new things. They simply felt they had no say in the matter. There was no co-creation, no being heard. It was being done to them. In contrast, Nik couldn't understand why they just didn't get it. I needed to tackle this one carefully.

My key hire was the Agile Coach. I needed someone who could balance out Nik, and maybe help him learn some new techniques as well. I needed someone who could gain the team's trust. Someone who would listen to their needs. Someone who would gently and carefully open the team up to see its own dysfunction, and then work on improving it. Someone who could truly coach (sweeping statement alert – 'most Agile coaches can't coach').

We'll call him Jem (yep, because it's also his name). His physical appearance was very different to the team (I do like a bit of disruption) but he cared deeply about how we introduced him to the team. A good sign. On his first day, at lunch, he chose to sit with the team rather than with me and my colleagues. I knew then that this would work. Within a few weeks the team had set him the task of learning all 40 of their names and particular pronunciations – a task that he took seriously, revising at home every night and earning kudos when they tested him.

Jem based his coaching around humanistic needs – assuming every behaviour is a response to a human need.

Sometimes we can get movement in behaviour by meeting the need in a different way. He carefully and gently helped the team introduce transparency to their work and address their continual improvement.

Nik had bounded across to me three weeks after Jem had arrived. 'Jem is great, isn't he!' he said.

'He is,' I replied. 'He's very different to you – I did that for a reason'.

'Oh' said Nik. It was at this point he realised Jem was as much for him, as for the team.

The pivot from *Follow me* Leadership to Humanistic needs based coaching and servant leadership was a key moment for the team. The team embraced many new practices and principles and this was reflected in their substantial performance improvement and team culture over a 9-month period.

On a side note, Jem and I tested my coaching hypothesis (aka sweeping statement) via many recruitment interviews together and we concluded that it's right – most agile coaches can't coach! Most can't even describe it correctly. My own confirmation bias was suitably nourished.

Nik developed hugely throughout the transformation via investment from his employer in skills training, working with Jem, and his own awareness. He has grown significantly as a leader. His *Emotional Intelligence* level is nicely topped up.

Insights

- Diversity of approach can balance out extremes.
  Look for different ways to tackle issues. There is no one right way – you need options.

- Leadership is changing. The leadership style of the past needs innovating and updating for modern world challenges.
  All the information is out there to be found.

- Coaching is powerful. Look beyond the behaviour to understand the human need that drives it. Learn to coach for performance – it is an incredibly powerful tool.

Pivot 2 – Don't fight culture – you always come off worse

"Company cultures are like country cultures. Never try to change one. Try, instead, to work with what you've got."

Peter Drucker

When we move to Scrum, one of the things we do is move to a team construct where no titles are recognised. It helps reduce the feel of hierarchy within the team that could spawn bad behaviours. Also, it focuses the team on everyone being committed to team outcomes, rather than individual activities. But what about when your title is important to you?

We saw this with the team. Nik had announced a flat structure with all team members being called developer. It's the way Scrum is commonly done, after all. The team were not happy. I was having lots of individual conversations. How would this work? How do I get promoted? How does my experience get recognised Have I lost all I have worked for to date? All great questions. The final straw came when a highly valued and knowledgeable developer resigned. How could it have got this bad?

I searched for answers and came across an interesting article – *'Why scrum doesn't work in Asia'.* Our team were predominately from the Indian subcontinent. It started to make us wonder. The importance of status and hierarchy in the culture. The expectation that the management has the answer. The preference for the title Project Manager over Scrum Master, due to assumed seniority from the term manager.

I'm a fan of Leandro Herrero's *Viral Change* techniques. He uses the informal network of influencers to initiate change.

We started to examine the influence network hiding in plain sight. We ignored the organisation chart – that was no use to us here. We needed to tap into the invisible network. We found three people who essentially ran the show for the team of 40. Highly experienced, highly knowledgeable. Everyone in the team looked to them for guidance and advice. If they were happy, everyone was happy. And we'd just taken their status away from them by assigning them the role of developer, same as everyone else. Facepalm.

We ended up doing something a bit anti-Scrum. We created an enablement team with these three principals. We retained their status and influence (actually by formalising it), but also worked on their behaviours. We worked with them to help the teams go faster. To share their knowledge and replace themselves. To guide the teams and ensure great outcomes, whilst downplaying individual heroics by them. It worked well. We tested new ideas with them. We introduced new ideas to the teams via the principals. We no longer had to influence 40 people to change. By working closely with these three people, to gain buy-in to new ideas, the larger teams followed.

The pivot here was away from Scrum *rules* and potentially fighting the culture – instead towards working with the culture. Some martial arts teach us to move and flow like water; "Regardless of the obstacles it encounters, water does not stop, it does not give up. It searches endlessly for the path of least resistance, and when there is none it rests, consolidating its power until it is time to rise up again."

Insights

- Culture is strong. Understand it and work with it to get change – don't clash with it head on.
- Find the influencers. They are the key to increasing the speed of change. Note: you won't find them listed on the Organisation Structure document.

Pivot 3 – Heretic to Backstage Management

"A new idea is first condemned as ridiculous and then dismissed as trivial, until finally, it becomes what everybody knows."

William James

Our role as leaders in transformation is to inspire change. We are often introducing external knowledge to people who have been relying solely on their experience and intuition for a long time.

Experience and Intuition are, of course, invaluable. They helped humans become the dominant species. Our ability to sense, categorise and respond based on experience and intuition makes us fast thinkers. But it also limits us. Experience is limited by the things we have done. Intuition is a belief system that we rarely challenge (it can also often be spectacularly wrong). So, Experience and Intuition don't help us change. In fact, they prevent us from changing. They are, after all, the things we know to be 'true'.

We need the addition of external knowledge to inspire change. That external knowledge could come from many places: reading, videos, observation, conversation, increased awareness, coaching, discovery, analysis, experimentation etc.

In the early days of the product transition above, during my introductions to the team about Lean/Agile/DevOps, I often felt like a heretic. My external knowledge challenged their experience and intuition. In these instances, it's easy for people to reject this received wisdom in favour of the things they *know to be true*. The concepts were openly ridiculed when I suggested automated provisioning of environments (they were used to a minimum of 6 weeks) and automated regression testing taking less than an hour (they were used to 328 man hours of manual testing).

Galileo said, "We cannot teach people anything; we can only help them discover it within themselves". How true. Many of my team coaching techniques rely on people discovering that their experience and intuition is limited in some way. Only after this self-discovery do they become receptive to new ideas.

The real secret to the success of this project-to-product management transition was the incumbent leadership. As consultants, we should never try and lead transformation from start to end. My role as chief dissident and nonconformist quickly changed to a role as a curious and slightly mad Sensei, and eventually on to a role as Backstage Manager, scheduling, coordinating and ensuring a great production (whilst hiding in the shadows). The real stars of the show were the leaders and the team. We rapidly stopped mentioning the name of the Transformation Programme, the narrative was about the team themselves (supported by the transformation). The leaders led from the front, inspiring the teams and rewarding continual improvement. Interesting blogs appeared on the intranet from team members. Big room planning sessions became community events with people bringing in home cooked food to share at lunch. They found their sense of purpose. The metrics spoke for themselves. I felt so proud of this team.

This pivot was from Transformation Lead – all new ideas and inspiring rhetoric – to Backstage Manager to the team and the incumbent leaders.

Insights

- Transformation works best when it is embedded within the incumbent leaders and the teams to continue their journey. Transition your role from transformation lead to backstage manager at the right moment. There are no medals for you. Get used to it.

- Help people self-discover the limitations of their experience and intuition. Only then can you introduce external knowledge. Systems thinking and causal loop diagrams are a great way of helping people discover the adverse effects of their best intentions.

- Create an environment for continual improvement. Make time, resources and recognition all reinforce the expectation to experiment, learn and improve.

Summary

In each of these scenarios above, the initial approach was found to be insufficient. New insight and options emerged as we progressed and a fundamental pivot was required. You cannot know these emerging approaches in advance, but we can expect them to happen. Of course, that's what makes it interesting.

About Adrian Stalham

Adrian Stalham is a *Partner* at *Sullivan & Stanley (S&S)* with experience across many different industry sectors.

He has a background in the traditional delivery of large projects and programmes, covering areas such as business transformation, *Omni* channel, organisation design, contact centres, B2B and B2C.

These days he is more commonly involved in Agile and lean ways of working, culture change, helping organisations adapt to complexity and coaching executives. Adrian strives to learn new things every day.

Outside of work, Adrian amuses himself creating an experience-based learning environment for his children and has interests in motorbikes, photography and clay pigeon shooting.

https://www.linkedin.com/in/adrian-stalham-97a6513/

Tell Me A Story

Jacqueline Shakespeare

Four simple words that evoke so many memories and emotions.

Humans are natural storytellers, we can't help telling stories. They are fundamental to our existence and my childhood was enriched by them. Enchanting, imaginary tales from my father about a field mouse and turtle who were the very best of friends and gritty stories of war time from my grandfather. My grandmother shared anecdotes of the people she had grown up with in Scotland. Charming, colourful characters, the memories of whom made her laugh as she told me the stories many years later.

I now read stories to my children and their desire for them is insatiable. They beg me to just finish the page, please, please and then as I do, will beg me for just one more. When our reading time eventually does end, they will immediately turn and pick up their own book, to lose themselves in a different world of adventure.

But how can stories help us in the workplace?

We consume enormous amounts of data every day through emails, instant messaging groups, documents, conference calls, newspapers, social networking sites, the list goes on. Our brains are constantly having to work out what information is useful and necessary and what they can let go of.

To be heard at work, we need to be original and compelling.

Facts and figures alone don't stick in our minds, but stories create sticky memories by attaching emotions to the rational information in front of us. Leaders who create and share strong stories have a powerful advantage.

When we tell stories well, we give the listener context and help them organise a mass of data into a form that is compelling and engaging. We create something that is memorable, repeatable and credible. It helps us to build a trusted relationship with the people we share our stories with.

So how can we develop our stories at work? The following principles will help you create your own engaging story.

Include context

To make sense of all of your information, people need to understand how everything fits together, the journey that you have been on so far and your current thinking. They will also benefit from a clearly articulated vision of where you are heading.

Add drama

When we experience an emotionally charged event, dopamine is released, making the story easy to remember. The brain is highly attracted to stories which involves a challenge with the promise of triumph in the end. Injecting drama into your story will help to drive belief in the need for change.

Make it personal

This will help individuals see the importance of their role in your journey and will give them a sense of purpose. People will come together through the shared experience you are offering them, making each individual feel part of something bigger. Ultimately, the more people identify with a story, the more open they are to being persuaded.

Be open and honest

Recognisable truth builds trust in the storyteller and credibility of the data being shared. People won't believe an over polished story, it will fail to engage your listeners.

Keep it simple

Simple stories are strong stories and the ones that captivate us the most. Remove any content in your stories that doesn't contribute directly to the narrative.

Embrace all learning preferences

Use visuals alongside the written word. Research has shown that the human brain processes images 60 times faster than words and that we remember visual images much easier and better than words. Narrate the story for your listener and, where possible, be physically together.

A while ago, I was working on an agile transformation in a UK based organisation. One day, the CFO called me into his office and said simply, 'I need your help'. It transpired that he was under pressure from the organisation's global parent company to confirm the business case supporting a new programme of work. He had to submit the business case by the first of the following month, just three weeks away.

The programme ambition was to move to a product centric operating model which enabled faster and more frequent delivery, more effectively, whilst maintaining quality.

This required transformational change to adopt the values, practices and tools for product development based on agility and DevOps.

A team of experts were helping the organisation to scope out the work. They had, in their view, comprehensively designed the ideal future state infrastructure and detailed out the supporting costs. They were therefore surprised when they took all of the data and information to the CFO that he felt it lacked credibility.

The CFO couldn't confirm the business case to the organisation's parent company because he didn't believe it and the programme team were unable to progress without the support of the CFO.

The CFO tried to explain he didn't understand where the numbers came from. The team of experts gave him more data, believing that was what he was asking for, but he wasn't. The transformation stalled.

I recognised that he was asking for a story. Simply having all the data, information, processes and practical solutions in place hadn't engaged him.

So, I brought everyone together. The external technical experts, members of the internal technology team, the HR and Finance teams and the Business Lead. A Business Lead that was leading in name only, a reluctant volunteer. It was clear to everyone in the room that he wasn't engaged.

Over a five-day period, we held a series of workshops and created our story, starting right at the beginning.

For the first two days, we didn't talk about technology at all. This was difficult and often uncomfortable for the infrastructure experts in the room. We worked through why we needed to change, we recognised our drama. We articulated our team purpose, vision and planned how we would make it relevant for people. I started to notice small changes in behaviour showing that people were beginning to engage in the transformation and move away from feeling that that change was just being done to them.

People's language became more inclusive, there were no more crossed arms and people were physically moving around the room so that they were closer to the work. The Business Lead voluntarily began to stand up to lead sections of the workshop. Whenever one of our key stakeholders dropped in (there was an open invitation to all of them), he was keen to be the one to share our progress and explain the new developments and thinking. Ownership for the change was starting to sit firmly with the Business Lead.

Finally, everyone understood why change was needed and was engaged in the ambition of the programme.

On Day three we started to look at the technology. We developed the future state infrastructure, understood what capabilities we needed and how we needed to structure the teams to deliver it all. Finally, we could start to build the cost model.

All the way through the process, I quietly kept stakeholders informed of our progress. I sent informal emails, the odd picture of people white boarding the future state infrastructure, all to build confidence in the work we were doing and to warm them up to the end story.

At the end of the five days, the team were exhausted but excited by the story that they had developed. All through the workshops we had been building the narrative, all of the thinking and detail had been captured, using words and visuals. When we left the workshop, the Business Lead had the completed story, ready to share with his stakeholders.

The Business Lead went to see the CFO. The CFO heard the story that he had been looking for, one that he felt was credible. The facts and data were still present, but the Business Lead's passion, ideas and opinions added perspective and believability. The CFO found the story persuasive, he engaged with the transformation and, finally, he could confirm the business case with the organisation's parent company and the team could move ahead with the transformation. The Business Lead told the story over and over again, across the organisation, to many different teams and individuals. The narrative was consistent and simple and therefore recognised and remembered.

He was no longer a reluctant volunteer, but an energised and engaged leader. The transformation was delivered successfully into the organisation and he has continued to tell stories ever since to engage and lead his teams through change. He understands that adults need stories as much as children do.

When you develop stories remember:

- Be consistent in your messaging and repeat often. Look at the problem through the eyes of your stakeholders rather than being driven by what you want to say.

- Remember that people are far more motivated by their organisation's transcendent purpose (how it improves lives) than by its transactional purpose (how it sells goods and services). Sharing personal stories makes you feel vulnerable, but it's that vulnerability that resonates with and connects you to other people.

- Flaws make stories interesting, more believable and more relatable. Never worry about creating the perfect narrative, just tell your story.

- Tell your stories with unflinching honesty, your listener will know if your story is genuine.

- Choose your storyteller well. The person who created the story isn't always the best narrator. Our feelings towards a storyteller influence our reaction to their story.

About Jacqueline Shakespeare

Jacqueline is a Partner at *S&S* with business and change expertise across the telecommunications, financial services and consultancy industries.

She specialises in technology transformations with a large customer impact and leading strategy definition, creating clear direction from a complex business challenge.

She is passionate about the people and engagement side of change, focussing on collaborative working, engagement and coaching. Jacqueline has leveraged the power of storytelling throughout her career to engage teams, create impactful messages and ultimately deliver change.

Away from work, she spends as much time as she can with her family, loves long country walks and exploring new countries.

https://www.linkedin.com/in/jacqueline-shakespeare-a8895312/

Going Tribal

Scott Potter

Let's begin at the end.

I was standing at the edge of our open-plan office area, watching the positive and varied interactions between the people, with a big smile on my face when a voice from behind me said, "You're a very lucky man... you can't teach that sort of passion and comradery."

I turned to see ... let's call him John ... *Macbook* in one hand and an *iPhone* being stroked by his thumb in the other, as glares at it shaking his head.

John had recently joined the business and was a senior stakeholder of some our my teams' software products. He had heard about our agile prowess, as one of his colleagues had apparently described us, and John had been curious ever since. To be honest, I wasn't sure how to take this description, I think it was meant as a compliment.

He made a few more remarks about his pains from working with prima donna agile teams in the past and continued on his way.

One of my staff had been watching, walked up to me and said, "We've come a long way haven't we."

We had. It certainly hadn't always been like this.

This environment and culture had been three years in the making and to be honest this trusting, productive and harmonious environment was still a little fragile ... it still needed protecting. The productivity and value creation had been decent for a while, but it had only recently been driven from within the teams ... and from the interactions between the teams.

It hadn't been a straightforward transformation. I needed to live by agile principles, because I didn't have all the answers at the start and things hadn't always gone right the first time. *Inspect & Adapt* or ... *Test & Pivot*, with a healthy sprinkling of creative problem solving, had been an essential ingredient throughout.

This chapter reflects on a time when I focussed on bringing about changes in behaviour, en masse.

It's about *Culture, Citizenship* and *Leadership*.

Culture

Culture is a heavily used word, especially when talking about agile transformations and business improvements. Culture is defined in many ways. To get some sort of handhold on this thing called *Culture*, I consider it a sum of collective behaviours which is a culmination of ones:

- Goals and Motivations
- Values and Beliefs
- Perspective and Interpretation

... and more.

This helped me approach the challenge of *Cultural Change* in the following way. To change or create a *Culture* is to change or align behaviours. In order to change a person's behaviours, this person has to gain new knowledge for their drivers of behaviour I mention above, to change.

To do this they need to be open to noticing, absorbing and synthesising new information.

Some people are clearly open-minded, others less so. But I now believe that even those who seem closed, actually absorb enough new information every day that they can adapt (or be adapted) to a new culture and therefore help reinforce that desired culture. We had many closed-minded and extremely opinionated people at the start of this journey.

Daily life is rich with sources of new information and the most valuable can often be found in the workplace, especially if it is a workplace that has aspirations of leveraging lean and agile principles to create high performing teams, as we had. These valuable sources may be in the form of differences of opinion, in one's blind spot and the other side of one's cognitive biases. For one to tap into them we often need others to help us become aware of them.

Citizenship & Leadership

Citizenship is about being a member of a collective, ideally providing one with a feeling of belonging, and behaving in a way that others expect you too. I wanted to break the deeply entrenched hierarchical mindsets and the mis-association of leadership being the preserve of those with authority or seniority. So I rolled citizenship into leadership for this particular transformation.

My TOPP Agility model

For these three years, I had a strategy that ensured we didn't over focus on one area of transformation at the expense of another. What I mean by this is that the technical foundations had to be in place and the right engineering practices being followed, to ensure that all the teams were capable of a fast turnaround time and able to release quickly, confidently and sustainably to production. There is little business benefit from implementing scrum ceremonies if you can't actually test ideas or incrementally build and release your product.

Likewise, even with a sound *Technology* foundation and development practices in place, if the principles underpinning our *Product* development and (dare I even use the term) *Project Management* processes were wrong, and the processes themselves couldn't provide ample feedback loops that increased our knowledge of options; progress; correctness and verification of value, then we still wouldn't be able to exhibit the speed and agility that I was determined to achieve.

Indeed, we may be pair-programming and conducting peer-reviews, but if people didn't feel comfortable giving difficult feedback to each one of their teammates, we wouldn't get the benefits of such practices.

Or conversely, if we grew the soft skills of each individual to be able to drive higher standards and help make their team a high performing team, but we hadn't dealt with the organisational issues to get the right level of delegated decision making authority into the team, then we still wouldn't be able to adapt or pivot quickly. Agility has several cornerstones of excellence ... *Technical, Organisational, Process* and *Personal* were the ones that I used for the TOPP agility model which helped us retain a suitably balanced portfolio of change initiatives.

Most of the time it was a natural process of listening, observing and planning areas to improve. But there was one incident which needed a significant *Pause, Intervention & Pivot.*

Something Went Wrong

About six months before John caught me enjoying my moment of reflection and pride, one of my *Scrum* teams went *Tribal.*

Tribal? What does this mean?

It all started about 12 months earlier when I had been working with a Life Coach and Management trainer to design a programme of *Soft Skills* development to support this agile transformation. A life coach? Why?

Progress So Far

By this point in our transformation we had Permanent teams, not project teams, Xp based development practices, a scrum based *Product Development* framework, bleeding edge cloud based infrastructure with pop-up environments and a slick CI/CD pipeline. Lean software development principles guided our ongoing decision making and some degree of entrepreneurial thinking was growing within our teams that we had managed to get a high degree of delegated decision making authority into.

Whilst my main change agents and I had made good progress in most areas of the TOPP Agility model, there still wasn't enough leadership being demonstrated (not the type of leadership that creates people who wait to be lead by the leaders, but situational leadership and people willing to take responsibility). There were still dominant individuals and others too quiet.

There was still too little passionate, constructive debate. And certainly too few of these debates resulting in meaningful outcomes and action.

We had good scrum masters who helped overcome all of this, but I wasn't content with that. There were still too few examples of peers having difficult but necessary conversations to hold one another accountable for their actions, or lack of action.

People would help one another and there was a degree of mentoring from some of the most experienced, but the skills to develop and grow their teammates through coaching techniques was noticeably absent.

I passionately believe that self organising, high performing teams need all their team members to be just as adept at interpersonal skills as they are at software design, monitoring and telemetry design, and setting up build & deployment pipelines.

With my main change-agents, I had to face into the need for this situation to change, and whilst we had been chipping away at it person by person, moment by moment (and trying to model this behaviour ourselves), it really needed a more comprehensive approach. *The Personal Agility Programme* was conceived

Why did I take this *Personal Excellence* aspect of an agile transformation on if our scrum masters were helping all teams to be sufficiently performant?

I wanted to make this transformation a real transformation, permanent and resilient... resilient to the remaining corporate and wider organisational issues that constantly challenged and chipped away at this bubble of commitment, trust and ownership behaviour. And more recently, in the *Standish Groups' 2015 Chaos Report*, I've found another way to answer this question.

20 Years of Agile

So 20 years after the emergence of several software development methodologies which challenged traditional project management thinking - and despite some naysayers - it turns out that delivering products in short cycles so that we can get more user involvement and faster feedback, continual improvement, and being able to efficiently adapt to new information and changing requirements, is infact a better way of delivering software projects and products. Really? Who'd have thought it?

However, transforming companies and teams to work in this way still seems to be a challenge. In fact, according to the *2015 Chaos Report* an improvement from 16% to 29% success rate of projects has been achieved. Certain projects were as high as 62%.

Through 2015 the report studied 50,000 projects around the world, from the small to the enormous. It also included some much needed changes to the criteria for defining success. So it's a valuable insight.

If projects and product developments were really being run in ways true to agile principles and values, surely the success rate would be higher. I think one of the reasons it's not, is due to the missing behaviours that I had identified as being essential.

'But where's the pivot?' I hear you ask. It's coming.

Back to the Personal Agility Programme

I started by identifying the vital behaviours that I wanted to develop and foster across all of my teams. At this point in time I had about 70 in my in-house team, 40 of which were permanent employees.

So, the team that went tribal... *The Product Owner* (PO), let's call him Mark, a nice guy, pretty good knowledge of agile techniques and has been a bit of a journeyman around London. He's seen good and bad adoptions of *Scrum* and many an environment that was meant to be living agile values.

The product was a paid-for product, part of a small digital product portfolio of a household brand, and a significant revenue stream for our business.

Mark was in a tough position, he didn't truly own the P&L budget and wasn't able to get his hands on all the levers that a *Product Owner* needs in order to take full ownership and accountability along with the rest of the scrum team. The person who had recently moved into the real, chief PO role - although not by job title - didn't really understand how technology could drive new revenue opportunities, nor how users of these digital products had different expectations to their traditional products. We had had a reasonably successful two years of Digital Transformation, faster speed to market of new products and features, fewer production incidents, reduced development costs and increased revenue from these releases, were all measurable improvements.

Our new technologies, skills and focussed efforts were providing greater value. However, recent senior personnel changes had accidentally derailed it. And this accidental creation of a Chief PO was one of those changes. Decision making had been pulled back up to a higher level of management outside of our business unit.

So the team were feeling frustrated and not in control of their own success. In fact, feeling decidedly hampered by the direction given by this senior person.

However, even before this change, the *Product Backlog* had barely covered more than the next sprint. For a while now, there had been no outcome-based roadmap nor strategic context to build a strong sense of purpose or to help the team use its initiative effectively.

This team had been very productive in the past and had been recognised as one of our more mature agile teams, passionate, capable, independent and delivering real value every sprint. Mark wasn't with them back then.

In recent times however, they were feeling powerless to make change and to improve the situation themselves. Mark was bearing the brunt of this.

We had already designed part of this *Personal Agility Programme* to help people realise that they aren't powerless and that they can make a difference. We had focussed on awareness and reflection:

- Taking responsibility for one's actions, and just as importantly one's lack of action.

- By noticing when something is wrong, to recognise that this as a possible opportunity to act, and

- Having the right interpersonal skills to be able to act, to influence, to raise difficult subjects, to have healthy conflict and to be able to move forwards constructively.

The Pivot

All was progressing well. We had staff feedback ranging from those who couldn't see the relevance of these *Experiential Learning Interventions* (there were few), to those lapping up every last drop of information, inspiration and practice opportunities.

So what went wrong? And why the pivot? Well, in truth, we had been tweaking the contents of each course module based on our own observations and feedback from the previous sessions. Something that worked very well was to run the modules with two groups, so we could even adapt before running the same module the second time.

We had planned the topics and outcomes in a way that we could evolve the course content whilst providing enough clarity about the entire course programme. We were *keeping up on our toes* or, *on the bounce* as a sports coach might say, to remain nimble and responsive. And it was fortunate that we did.

This particularly frustrated team, seeing no strategic thinking and even worse, feeling that their last two sprint's releases had added no business or customer value, were at their wits end. Mark was feeling less in the team and more isolated.

But with the following words ringing in their ears from their recent course module, they decided to take matters into their own hands.

You can ALL make a difference. *Notice - Decide - Have Courage - Act.*

I got wind of, what was being referred to as a *Mutiny*.

The team had decided not to attend the sprint planning session, setting their own sprint goal. Several extremely heated exchanges between PO and team members in our open-plan office, were what made up a very emotional and volatile week.

I, of course, found myself involved as a senior member of staff with a team exhibiting completely unacceptable behaviour. Together, we resolved the immediate issue, getting the team (including Mark) working together again.

The main pivot was to prioritise the learning and practicing of behaviours above the morale boosting, motivational self-awareness concepts of empowerment and leadership.

At the beginning of the entire journey, *The Culture*, if I could call it that, wasn't particularly conducive to building respect or trust among co-workers across any levels of the Organisation. So as well as increasing our Technical capabilities to be able to deliver quality solutions which built trust and respect from our stakeholders, we needed to ensure that our staff had the skills to be able to have the right kind of interactions in order to create an environment ... a micro-climate in which they could thrive ... wanting to strive for better, to try new things, openly reflect and learn from their experiences, to set themselves high standards and to be able to hold one another accountable for achieving them.

The irony of this episode was that I had decided to take on the challenge of why people weren't stepping up to lead and challenge the status quo because 1) they didn't feel it was safe to do so; and 2) didn't believe that they could actually make a difference.

We had given them some belief, the will to act, but not necessarily the skills to be able to do so effectively.

For peers to hold one another accountable, many things need to be in place. So to recap, to help everyone realise that they aren't powerless and that they can make a difference, we focussed on:

- Taking responsibility for one's actions, and just as importantly one's lack of action.

- Recognising when there is an opportunity to act, and

- Having the right interpersonal skills to be able to act, to influence, to raise difficult subjects, to have healthy conflict and to be able to move forwards constructively.

- Leadership is not about authority.

In the end, the powerless found they had the power to make changes. And eventually they were also equipped with the personal tools to do so constructively and responsibly.

So two and a half years after initiating a substantial agile transformation, 12 months after facing into the cultural and behavioural issues head-on, 6 months after one team had gone tribal and one minute after *Macbook* carrying, *iPhone* stroking John's remarks, I was feeling rather proud of where we had got to. The starting point, as well as the nature of the journey, is what made this transformation all the more rewarding.

About Scott Potter

Scott Potter MSc is a Software and Product Development professional, educated to MSc level, with two decades of experience specialising in software development, building on previous product development and R&D experience.

Learning and using Lean principles in the early 1990s - specifically Kanban - to increase flow and reduce cycle time, Scott took this into software development. Incremental and evolutionary development models have been used throughout this time.

In more recent times, through his *Value Flow Solutions Consultancy*, Scott has tailored many tools and strategies to help large and small companies change their culture and technology stacks to become more nimble and productive.

Scott says, "I was fortunate to work with and learn from many of the pioneers in our field such as James Grenning, Bob Martin and Craig Larman. I remember how they inspired me to think differently, to aspire for better... much better. I want others to experience this contagious enthusiasm and I try to do my bit for our profession, in any little way that I can."

Scott had been pioneering many agile practices behind closed doors at Xerox throughout the 2000s. January 2012 saw Scott start to bring this expertise out into our community.

https://www.linkedin.com/in/scottpotteruk/

www.ValueFlowSolutions.co.uk

scott@valueflowsolutions.co.uk

"We Know They're Meaningless But You Have To Do Them Anyway"

A Case Study About Eliminating Timesheets

Brett Ansley

In 2015, I was working with a European online fashion retailer to help restructure and coach them to help improve their software delivery. The organisation had experienced a phenomenal 15 years of double-digit growth. But they had realised that their technology costs were growing at the same rate as their revenue. The way they were structured was not scaling well. To meet their aggressive future growth plans, they would need to change the way they were structured in order to scale more effectively.

A central *Programme Management Office (PMO)* of nine programme managers was managing all the development work. Requests for changes or new functionality would come into them; they had a master plan of what all the developers were currently working on and what they were due to be working on for the foreseeable future. Requests were planned into the system and developers allocated. A budget was sent to finance and agreed. The assigned developers were required to work to the agreed budget. Developers were tracked through their submission of time-sheets at half hourly granularity.

Timesheets were universally hated by the development teams. They were the only department in the whole organisation which needed to enter timesheets, and for them, it was a chore that took away precious time from writing software while adding no appreciable value. On average they were spending an hour a week completing timesheets so not only was it a universally despised process, it was also an expensive one.

Federica led the *PMO* – she was stressed and overworked. She knew this was not the best way to work, and she had some great ideas about how things could be better, but she didn't feel empowered to make any change.

Working with Federica and her team we created a set of stable cross-functional teams to start handling the work rather than arbitrarily allocating work to groups of developers. We also talked to the developers about pair programming and collaborative creation. The teams all wanted to be more collaborative about how they created and were keen to work together and with others to build on and enhance the product, but the timesheet system didn't allow them to have two people working on the same task at the same time.

I spoke to Finance about how they used the information generated from the budgeting process and the timesheets. It turned out the budgets were used to create financial forecasts for capital growth and amount of expenditure (as tasks within projects were allocated to either Capital Expenditure (CapEx) or Operational Expenditure (OpEx). These growth and expenditure forecasts formed part of the presentation to the markets about the future financial position of the company.

Timesheet information was then used to calculate the actual position of the company on a month-by-month basis, and this was then reconciled to the forecast. On a quarterly basis the forecast and actual figures were reported to the markets. Finance was concerned that any change in the way this information was created, managed or reported could mean that the market reports were incorrect or it could lead to actuals differing from forecasts and this could have a significant impact on the share price. Any adverse impact on the share price was unacceptable to the business.

That meant we needed to figure out how to change the system in such a way that it had little or no impact on the information that flowed into Finance. Or that, at the very least, change was staggered in such a way so as to keep the actuals in sync with the previous quarter's forecasts and growth consistent with the annual *CapEx* forecast. This was no mean feat.

Federica and I did some detective work on the timesheet data. It turns out that developers typically had some problems entering data into the timesheet system. The system expected them to enter at least 8 hours of time each day to project work. This meant that meetings, ad-hoc conversations and other day-to-day activities had no place. Also, developers were allocated to multiple projects at any one time and also had responsibility to fix bugs coming back from previous work they had done. At the end of the day, it was hard for them to work out (with any kind of accuracy) how much time they had spent on any of the given tasks.

The developers needed to make a judgement call; they could go through the process of trying to find the right bucket for each and every activity and asking for buckets to be created where there weren't any, but this process took a significant amount of time. Instead, they put ambiguous time against project budgets that they knew would get approved. Also, if there was work they knew needed to be done but would never get a budget allocation, they would put this into the budget for a project that would definitely get approved. This reduced the time they allocated to budgets they knew were under scrutiny.

The developers in this situation were not trying to swindle the company, they were genuinely trying to do the best thing, but they didn't have the right buckets available to them to allocate work to and were also keenly aware of how they needed to limit the overall impact to the financial forecast. Within the constraints of the system, they were doing the best they could.

Armed with this information, I went back to Finance. I asked them if we could streamline the process to reduce the reliance on timesheets – given that we knew that timesheets were inaccurate. The Finance team agreed that the timesheets were inaccurate and that this was something they were aware of. But for them this was not so much of an issue – the key point for them was that an individual (not in Finance) had signed-off to the fact that this work had been done and had taken the indicated time. This way when an auditor questioned a figure they were able to produce a verifiable paper trail for how the figure was calculated. From their point of view while accuracy was good, auditability was critical, and reducing the reliance on timesheets would mean they would lose their audit trail.

Now we needed to come up with a solution that did not adversely impact the financials and would provide Finance with the same degree of auditability, but would also free up the developers from having to create timesheet entries that didn't accurately reflect the work they had done.

We created a process whereby the team leads would record who was working on their team each day (at half day granularity), and this report would be sent to Finance as an auditable and verifiable artefact.

The next artefact sent to Finance was a record of all the items of work that a team completed in a given week. Each item of work was marked as either *CapEx* or *OpEx* so that we could report on the proportion of that team's output that was *Capital* vs. *Operational* expenditure, and what proportion of the team's time was applied to the various projects. This formed the second auditable and verifiable artefact signed off by the *PMO*.

The final piece of the puzzle came from HR – this was the daily cost of each individual. Knowing the daily cost of each individual, which individuals worked on which teams, and what proportion of time each of those teams dedicated to *CapEx* vs. *OpEx* allowed us to calculate the value of the work split by team and type of expenditure and by project, and this could then form part of the financial statements.

We agreed to run the two processes in parallel for one quarter so that we could ensure that there was no significant difference in the output and to allow the transition in market forecasts to take place. As it turned out, the computed values were more consistently in line with the forecasts than the self-reported amounts, and after two months we agreed to stop self-reporting.

As in any change programme there were people who were very sceptical of the overall programme of change and some of the developers were not keen on the changes that were being introduced, but the death of the timesheet was a significant win for them, and it helped to win the sceptics over, giving us more chance to improve.

About Brett Ansley

Brett is a leading advocate of lean thinking, the application of *Kanban* and the use of quantitative techniques in delivering high-quality, digital products that delight customers and generate revenues. A pioneer in his field, Brett has a vast network and considerable influence across social media platforms, leading the way as an *Agile Lean Kanban Coach.*

He is a versatile coach, executive mentor, and change driver. He has worked with blue-chip companies such as *lastminute.com, SkyScanner;* and Government. Brett helps companies:

- Reduce the time to market for digital services
- Recover from failed Agile Transformations
- Improve delivery predictability and risk analysis

When businesses:

- Are constrained by the speed of delivery of their technology and digital services; Brett improves efficiency through delivery capability.
- Have tried to go *Agile* but are not seeing expected benefits; Brett will manage risk to improve predictability and increase revenue.
- Technology/digital services delivery is unpredictable, or you see you are lagging behind your competitors; Brett will create organisational agility.

Brett has an outstanding track record of success coaching businesses, providing strategic direction, intervening on struggling projects, mentoring through Lean techniques, and delivering growth and revenue.

https://www.linkedin.com/in/bransley/

Peer Hubs: An Evolutionary Journey Towards Peer Hubs

Wayne Palmer

In 2014, *Peer Hubs* became the basis of a new operating model for a data and analytics consultancy in Melbourne, Australia. Replacing the previous line management hierarchy, *Peer Hubs* were designed to operate as small, collaborative networks; each equipped to help their members express their needs, learn, and feel connected to a common purpose.

Peer Hubs were not the original intent however – they were the result of the organisation attempting to replace their performance appraisal system. Through listening, learning and adaptation it proved possible to find an answer to a much bigger question - what kind of company do I want to be a part of?

Many hats

The consultancy was less than ten years old and had established itself across Australia as a result of its people, all of whom were highly talented, independently-minded, authentic individuals. My background in transformational initiatives resulted in me having an external and internal job title; *Principal Consultant* and *Head of People and Culture* respectively.

The internal title was borne out of genuine concern from the CEO; when larger companies approached them with an offer, our people were often lured away. How do you create a company where people are intrinsically motivated to stay? What can we do about it? As a result of its rapid growth there was no coherent operating strategy in the company, no sense of higher purpose. This is typical in many organisations; structures, processes and practices had been borrowed from other companies and combined with hasty trains of thought to create what resembled a functioning system.

This approach creates a significant amount of *organisational debt*[1], which all companies experience to some degree. What was unusual was finding a CEO willing to fully acknowledge this, and be willing to accept new ideas and approaches in resolving this debt.

Through my initial conversations with consultants in a number of locations I discovered two common sources of internal friction. The process for requesting leave had multiple levels of approval combined with a large degree of frustration, and everyone hated the performance appraisal system.

The annual appraisal of individual performance is at best meaningless, and at worst humiliating and demoralising. It is one of the destroyers of culture, one of the deadly diseases[2] of traditional management. The one in use at the consultancy was genuinely frightful, with seven tabs of *Microsoft Excel* needing completion. The output was used in promotion and pay discussions and was rarely completed until the last minute due to pressures from client work.

It became obvious through a few simple conversations that changing the performance appraisal system would make a genuine difference to how the consultants viewed the organisation. What was not obvious at the time was just how much else would need to change as a result.

A spark at speed dating

Senior management within most organisations are typically presented with a slice of the corporate hierarchy to manage. Within my care were managing consultants, who looked after senior consultants, who looked after consultants. There are a number of reasons for these matryoshka doll hierarchies to exist, most are rarely valid.

Within this particular consultancy, the reasoning was administrative; to ensure compliance of company policy and complete the performance appraisal each year.

A budget was provided to consultants in order to meet their subordinates for coffee in the city, to ask how life was, to remind them of upcoming work events and then to get back to their client sites. It was at best uninspiring. People rarely showed up, citing client work pressures and deadlines, and as the deadline for performance appraisal completion approached people began feeling more disengaged and frustrated with the organisation.

An intervention was needed. I asked my consultants for permission to invite everyone within our part of the hierarchy to come and take part in a big speed dating retrospective. Speed dating is, I am led to believe, an opportunity for people to come together and explore emotional fit in a short space of time. The language seemed oddly appropriate, and made people curious to attend.

The retrospective was a facilitated workshop designed to explore our life goals and priorities and uncover what help (if any) was needed from the group or the broader company. I was curious to find out who we all were, how we would react when together and how much vulnerability we could demonstrate.

Vulnerability was crucial within this exercise. It is typically the first thing people look for in each other, and the last thing you hope anyone sees in yourself[3].

As the nominal head of this hierarchy, it was critical for me to go first and demonstrate vulnerability to the group so that they had a degree of *emotional permission* to do the same. I pre-populated my entries during the setup of the room and talked it through with everyone at the start. The aim was for authentic, open conversation to transpire.

The response was amazing. We talked for hours about the difference between extrinsic wants and genuine, intrinsic needs. One consultant shared that what he really valued was close personal relationships at work. Another recognised she had no real career goal; how her desire to become a home owner in a challenging property market was consuming her every waking moment.

Displaying genuine, authentic vulnerability with people is an act of trust. It provides the foundation for every organisation to make dramatic leaps in performance, by enabling people at every level to share their needs, hopes and challenges. It allows an organisation to learn.

We learned more about each other in this exercise than would have been possible in a hundred coffee meet ups. There are critical moments during any transformation; a story which can be shared and used as a catalyst for further, deeper change. The approach we had taken and the result achieved had real merit. The next challenge was to take that learning and use it as a platform to replace the performance appraisal system.

Performance appraisal to improvement canvas

The workshop triggered a burst of energy and intrinsic motivation which was to remain throughout the next 12 months. It is critical to identify your purpose and in this situation, mine was clear; by replacing the performance appraisal system the organisation could become healthier[4].

A new appraisal system would enable the company to learn

more about its people, to value their thinking and to act upon that thinking. I wanted to focus the organisation on learning about its people, not to distill its people down to a number for processing.

Discovering the *Mentor Canvas*[5] made the idea of a collaborative, mentorship approach appealing; the idea of finding a way of condensing the workshop exercise into a simple A3 format even more so. Several rounds of discussions with directors and the *control group* led to the production of an Improvement Canvas designed to generate as much valuable information as possible.

This A3 canvas had columns centred around *Self Reflection, Personal Improvement* and *Organisational Improvement*.

Feedback sessions with consultants saw a fourth column added called *Work Rating*; designed to help people rate experiences on client sites and whether their needs effectively aligned to the needs of the customer.

The four seasons of Autumn, Winter, Spring and Summer provided the perfect cadence, not too burdening for consultants and more natural than the previous yearly cycle aligned to the financial year. The *Improvement Canvas* was perfectly designed. Feedback had been gathered from all quarters, it's development iterated and validated with the control team. There was only one minor issue - *it was doomed to failure.*

The canvas was designed from the ground up to shape authentic conversations, and in order to be completed effectively it required a safe environment. Some sections were designed to be completed in solitude, some with a pair and some in a group. Creating enough safety in a group setting so people could be vulnerable was simply not possible across every city the organisation was located within. The control group had bonded as a result of this safety, but across the consultancy there was simply not enough trust to go around.

Pivot to Peer Hubs

According to 2009 research by *Edelman PR*, 57% of people trust their peers the most, especially when risk is involved[6] (in 2018 we see this eroding somewhat, especially on social and search platforms).

When time is short and risk is great, people turn to their peers – not to their managers. If we were going to have a meaningful, open and authentic conversation with each other we needed to have the canvas completed by and with peers, not within a manager/subordinate hierarchy.

In order to successfully replace the performance appraisal system, we would need to do something far more radical than previously imagined. At every level within the consultancy, we began to discuss how we could flatten the hierarchy and build trust. Peer Hubs were born.

An experiment was launched in January 2015 and was due to run for a season, when the organisation would assess the impact of introducing *Peer Hubs*. The original desire was to keep the experiment small (a single *Peer Hub* operating under the new approach), in effect legitimising the control team formed during the retrospective workshop. This was expanded to include a Peer Hub from each city to accommodate any cultural nuances we were unaware of. A set of guiding principles[7] were hypothesised, aiming to articulate the intent and help inform the design of any process.

While it was agreed there was to be no formal hierarchy, there remained a challenge. Someone was needed to help organise admin and logistics, be willing to put expense claims through at meet-ups and be the first to express themselves openly in order to help authentic dialogue to take place. Each *Peer Hub* needed someone willing to be vulnerable, first.

A *Peer Hub Facilitator* role was defined, and the intent of the role was discussed with people from across the organisation. This role and its attributes did not follow institutional hierarchy or introvert/extrovert lines - people with the ability to actively listen and trigger meaningful conversation were both present and a sent at every level. To provide the facilitators with a platform to work from, an intensive two-day workshop was devised where the importance of diversity, different learning styles and different facilitation techniques were introduced.

Those intensive two days were followed by continual flights between Melbourne, Sydney and Brisbane to coach, mentor and bring the experiment to life. The *Peer Hubs* were the focal point for much deeper, open conversations with or without the canvas. The conversation is what mattered most.

This activity and the feedback received to date led the directors to their conclusion - it was time to amplify the experiment.

Amplify the experiment

Is it possible that it is against the law to behave authentically within a company? HR consultants were brought in to validate that the change in approach was legal, considering our duty of care to our employees. The organisation was deemed OK from an external perspective, but the internal perspective was equally challenging. Bonuses and remuneration were all linked to performance evaluation and proved challenging to replace. Internal systems and processes all expected people to have a single manager as opposed to a group of peers, and those people were expected to be distilled down to a number.

The organisation was now actively engaged in both client work and organisational design, in pursuit of our guiding principles. People had an opportunity to craft both their career and their company. One *Peer Hub* sat down and listed out all of the touch points between a company and an employee to evaluate what each felt like; where did the organisation create positive or negative friction. Some touch points were missing altogether; an alumni system which previously did not exist was established with former colleagues joining a *Slack* channel. The organisation was beginning to resemble more of a community.

As the organisation moved closer to its transition, a self-selection exercise[8] was run where people within every city could choose which *Peer Hub* they wished to be in according to specific rules around diversity. Our built-in preference for associating with people like ourselves is natural but can serve to confirm our biases and limits learning. The *Peer Hubs* were designed to be learning vehicles, to help people step outside of their comfort zones and associate with people from different backgrounds, genders, cultures and needs. For consultants who were asked to operate on different client sites, it would give them a distinct advantage.

A decision was taken to have directors external from the *Peer Hubs* in the short/medium term to help with safety, so a *Foundation Hub* was established.

The purpose of the *Foundation Hub* was to flow valuable work into the organisation, and to remove challenges and issues raised by the *Peer Hubs*. Each city nominated a director to become a *State Facilitator*, and in the spirit of reverse delegation they picked up all of the things that the *Peer Hubs* no longer wanted to do – such as the leave process. The *Peer Hubs* decided to let the directors experience their frustrations with that particular process more fully.

New processes were defined to manage movement between *Peer Hubs,* a cadence was established for seasonal communication - but as much as possible the *Peer Hubs* were to autonomously decide their meetup frequency, rules and approach. They were provided a budget and additional coaching/training/logistics if requested. *Peer Hubs* became vehicles not only for learning, but as the basis for evolving the company based on continuous *Peer Hub* feedback.

Evolution over revolution

Over a 12 month period an organisation listened, adapted and launched a unique operating model designed to fit its particular needs perfect for that moment in its history. By following guiding principles and defining feedback cycles centred around systemic improvement, they became perfectly placed to respond to the needs of their people and build a genuine community of data and analytics professionals.

By keeping changes frequent and small, reverting back to the status quo never felt like an option - people's imagination had been captured, and the desire of every person to learn, grow and feel connected to a common purpose took hold.

References

1. Blank. S., *'Organisational Debt is like Technical debt – but worse',* 19 May 2015, https://steveblank.com/2015/05/19/organizational-debt-is-like-technical-debt-but-worse/ (accessed 2015)

2. Deming. W. (2000). *Out of the Crisis,* MIT Press.

3. Brown. B. (2012). *Daring Greatly,* Penguin.

4. Laloux. F. (2014). *Reinventing Organisations,* Nelson Parker.

5. Stairs. A., *'Design your mentor experience...The Mentor Canvas',* 23 July 2014, https://clunky.com.au/2014/07/23/design-your-mentor-experience-the-mentor-canvas/ (accessed 2014)

6. Peppers. D., Rogers M. (2012). *Extreme Trust,* Penguin.

7. Palmer. W., *'Peer Hub Resources',* http://www.open.works/peer-hub-resources/, 2018.

8. Mamoli. S., Mole. D. *'Self-Selection Kit'* http://nomad8.com/team-self-selection-kit/ (accessed 2014)

About Wayne Palmer

Wayne Palmer has spent the last two decades involved in software development, from start-ups to global enterprises.

Recognised by his peers as an expert in lean and agile principles and practices, during the past ten years Wayne has focused on business and digital transformation projects, guiding technology companies to be more effective and efficient by adopting new ways of working.

This transformative work spans public sector, logistics, telecoms and finance sectors across the UK, Europe and Australia and includes brands such as *Telstra, Australia Post* and *Vocalink.*

Through this work, Wayne has discovered the joy in helping establish organisations where trust, authenticity and engagement are the norm, thus assisting these humane organisations to exhibit huge potential in their respective markets.

To find out more about Wayne Palmer, his availability for consultancy work and speaking engagements you can drop him an email at being@open.works, Tweet him @waynerpalmer or look him up on *LinkedIn.*

https://uk.linkedin.com/in/waynerpalmer

How to Hire The Best

Matt Bradley

People, Process, Technology. The three words I typically hear when sitting down with a CxO to discuss their organisations change agenda.

"We need to improve them all."

Well, quite. This is undoubtedly true, but fundamentally it comes down to the *People*. Without the right people, without the right skills, mindset, culture, however you want to wrap it up. Without people you can trust, you can wave goodbye to improvements in the other two.

Great people are the most important part of any successful Transformation, Programme or Product Build. And having access to the right talent quickly to deliver is a close second. Whether you are introducing subject matter experts to co-create solutions with your internal capability, or deploying a whole new cross-functional team to deliver a product, access to the right skills, fast, is paramount.

To build powerful and high performing teams in today's skill-short and crowded marketplaces you must be able to compete and on-board resources efficiently.

Yet all too often I see large organisations being their own worst enemy, with HR, Procurement and low quality resource suppliers being major impediments to creating an agile workforce.

If I had a pound for every time I saw a broken *automated* workflow for recruitment over the last 12 years of my career. Taking ten days for multiple approvals by four layers of directorates, with hiring managers eventually having to chase requests manually through the system? Only then to be told the budget they have is £xxx under the market rate they need. It is nonsensical in today's skill-short markets, but an all too familiar tale.

Modern organisations should empower hiring managers to make quick decisions and take-action. They should be allies in streamlining outdated and broken processes. We must convince every part of the system to embrace Agile & Lean values in order to engage and energise the talent needed for sustainable change.

The good old days

It wasn't always like this. When I first entered the recruitment market in the mid noughties I have fond memories of partnering with some top FTSE investment banks and magic circle laws. These were massive enterprises, many layers of management, and large change agenda's. Yet when it came to bringing in skills to fill the capability gaps, there was minimal bureaucracy.

There were boundaries on how to engage and the old school quarterly / annual reviews, but by and large you could be proactive in responding to the needs of the business. I had some fantastic relationships based on trust. I had the opportunity to build relationships with hiring managers and the people at the coal face of change.

It worked. Regular communication and direct feedback, the ability to inspect and adapt to changing requirements was a recipe for success.

But, somewhere a lot of these large companies went a bit mad. Decisions around hiring started to be based on cost and not quality. The implementation of large *Preferred Supplier Lists (PSLs)*, tedious and clunky recruitment portals and worst of all, *Recruitment Process Outsourcing (RPOs)* ruined the flow. If you make low cost decisions, expect low quality returns.

The new world see's organisations outsourcing their people strategies or having multiple agencies competing for the same resources. Throwing CV's at recruitment portals hoping something will stick. Managers already under time pressure now have mountains of interview debt to deal with and more often than not, still don't get the resource they needed.

HR and Procurement functions historically work on annual or at best quarterly cycles. By nature these departments are not exposing key agile values of short cycles, regular reflection and course correction. When you add in PSLs, RPOs and clunky IT Systems you've got no chance of filling those capability gaps quickly with the best people.

One very large financial institution now claims to be on the largest global Agility Transformation in history, but recruitment and on-boarding processes takes at least 12 weeks for an interim. I spoke to one hiring manager who has been searching for a Business Analyst for 8 months through his RPO. Startups have built a product, ripped a hole in a traditional market and sold it for millions in eight months. The best resources do not have the patience nor are they on the market for long enough to endure such painful processes. Good people do not like being procured and the top 5% of resources are put off working for larger corporates by bloated recruitment processes.

Time to Pivot

Over time I became disillusioned with working for the larger corporates. I consciously pivoted towards the end of the noughties to partner with mid-sized and growing companies. Here I could continue to have strong relationships, be nimble, effective and responsive to the needs of my customer.

While getting in close with my clients looking to scale their tech teams over the last ten years, I watched the rise of Agile in their practices. They were becoming more product centric and customer focused. Building iteratively, improving collaboration, responsiveness and promoting a culture of continuous improvement and learning. I was seeing the teams I was building making dramatic improvements in the way they were working.

Now at *Sullivan & Stanley* we are instilling these same agile values. I am again partnering with some larger companies needing to change and compete with the new disrupters in their markets. We only work with organisations that are committed to improving the ways they work and let us operate in an Agile way.

We are constantly asking what does my customer need? What does my hiring manager need? We are proactive and coach clients to remove friction so we can have maximum effect.

So how can companies bring more agility, simplicity and flow to their hiring processes? Here's my top ten insights:

1. **Break down barriers:** Literally and physically you need suppliers and operations to be a true part of the cross functional team, so position them as such. I typically spend a day on site every two weeks with my clients. Incorporating myself into retrospectives, communities of practice and contributing to the planning process.

2. **Build relationships**: Talk and spend time getting to know your operational teams and suppliers, take them for lunch, share videos, podcasts and articles. Develop understanding and trust in what you are trying to achieve. You need advocates if you're going to attract the best people.

3. **Work in Sprints**: Be proactive. For every new set of requirements implement a two week sprint.
Work with your trusted partner to communicate clear deliverables and block time out in your diary so these are met. At *S&S* we tend to bring our sponsors in for a whole afternoon to meet with a selection of our associates, thus reducing the interview debt and getting the right result.

4. **Focus on empowerment:** Improve collaboration and communication and drive self-service to ensure processes and systems enable teams to move faster. Encourage a culture of empowerment for Hiring Managers - give them the opportunity to hire the best talent on the market.

5. **Get Alignment:** HR focus on process and efficiency, procurement on cost, hiring managers on quality - a fundamental misalignment of departments is the outcome. All three need to be aligned on the outcome required for the Organsiation to get the skills needed.

6. **Find trusted partners:** Those that have an innovative approach and can help attract the best tech and change agents to your organisation. The best suppliers only work with clients exclusively and you will get much better results from having a close trusted relationship.

7. **Implement Retrospectives:** Hiring Managers, Suppliers and Operations should be meeting regularly to talk about skill gaps, market conditions and impediments. The more proactive you can be to market pressures the better equipped you will be to optimise the process and succeed.

8. **Improve the Flow:** Less focus should be on the quarterly or annual reviews of suppliers and more emphasis on

continuous feedback and improvement. This will enable better performance and the continuous delivery of great people into your programmes. Long tender processes are not in line with the fast paced world of technology and business.

9. **Think about quality over cost:** Is Procurement basing their decisions based on market conditions? In today's world they should be adopting greater degrees of adaptability. Squeezing your best suppliers margins because they have closed a number of capability gaps feels like punishment for a job well done, and does not encourage further collaboration and transparency.

10. **Adopt an Agile mindset:** Communicate with suppliers in a more open way, be forward thinking and adapt to the market conditions - take back control and don't rely on the best thinking from ten years, or even one year ago.

Be Brave

We must remove the fear and change our attitudes to business. Companies that strive to hire the best talent for their programmes are half way on the journey to being an Agile organisation. The focus should be getting the right individuals to fit your culture and coach your existing teams in better ways of working. Hiring the best is the most simple way to achieve greater agility. People with the right mindset, skill-set, attitude and desire to delight your customers.

Change the structure, remove impediments and improve agility. It's easy to say, but harder to practice. Executives need to be brave. It requires strong leadership and management to go against the grain and do what is best. These are tough decisions, but surely not as tough as not having the right calibre people delivering the change your business needs.

About Matt Bradley

Matt Bradley has been at the forefront of Technology and Business Change recruitment for over 12 Years. He has partnered with organisations across the UK, Europe and Australia and built high performing teams for the likes of *Panasonic, DHL, The Press Association* and *Mastercard.*

Matt is the Organiser of the agility community that co-created this book and enjoys bringing people together to share stories. He is passionate about driving deeper engagement with talent communities through knowledge sharing, crowdsourcing and community driven events.

Since 2016, Matt has help build *Sullivan & Stanley*, a premiere top 5% crowd company for senior technology and change interims, designed to transform and future proof organisations.

Matt is married to Celine with a beautiful baby girl, Martha.

https://www.linkedin.com/in/mwbradley/

Agility In a Complex Organisation

Bhavesh Vaghela

I joined a digital agile program 150 miles away from home. My alarm was set for 4am, my flowery shirt was ironed, the car was fuelled, and the Spotify play list was ready!

On my first day I managed to avoid the M6 car park and get to work early. I was welcomed by a trendy office with lots of busy people jumping on calls. On the surface the programme looked healthy. It had all the right people: BAs, UX, UI, copy writers, infrastructure engineers, developers, testers and PMs. The teams were dotted around the UK and offshore.

As a hobbyist mechanic my father used to say, 'What you see or hear on the surface does not usually really reflect reality. To truly understand what's going on you have to lift the bonnet and test your assumption.'

I started to read through the reporting packs to understand on timelines and workstreams. The program was green with a few dots of amber and all looked normal-within range and healthy. This was far from the truth in reality. The project was actually in trouble and required intensive care! To understand what was going on under the bonnet and get some situational awareness I mapped out the core teams and all the sub teams. I created a mind map of the teams and added one word to describe what they did. Where possible I included any apparent connections or handoffs.

As I talked to each team, I discovered a matrix of handoffs across the teams with each having a different understanding on what they were delivering. This is a key symptom when the mission and objectives of the teams are not aligned.

When teams are not aligned with a clear mission and objectives, assumptions are made about who is doing what. You end up with duplication of work, big gaps in delivery, and heavy-handed programme management. In some places it is possible to see five Project Managers managing one developer! Thinking about the overall end-to-end business design is key; value streaming mapping helps here to ensure each part of the process adds value to the outcome. Without this the outcome will be ineffective delivery. Arms and legs are fitted into bits of work that need to be done, then more people are bought in to fill the gaps to make the program wheels turn. It's like having a car that is using too much fuel: the long term solution is never to go to the petrol station more often.

Another thing I see when team objectives are not aligned is a turf war about who owns the work. Knowledge is power and that leads to insular teams who work harder to protect their domain than delivering customer value. These teams tend to not share anything of value with the wider project team in the fear that they will lose power, and more importantly, they tend to not declare any mistakes or lessons learnt.

I requested from each team a brief synopsis of the goals of the team and for what they were responsible. On paper this sounds like a great idea to get a common understanding. In reality, however, it didn't work. I received *War and Peace* from some teams, a few bullets points from others, so it was impossible to figure out what was more valuable and where there was overlap. Work is dynamically complex where one output determines the next input; tacit work and operational hacks get things done but are difficult to unearth.

We had to try something different! I ran a number of face

to face workshops with all the teams where we talked about what each team did and their self-perceived purpose in the programme. Focusing on the why provides an abstract of day to day tasks, helps drive clarity, and makes alignment possible.

My top tips are:

- Have plenty of breaks and provide lunch so people can share bread with each other and interact. I would say it is as equally, if not more important, for teams to know each other personally than it is to understand what each other's team do.
- Avoid using the Transformation word. Change is the hardest thing to do and I find if you use the T-word people tend to become defensive and despondent.
- Use words such as continuous improvement or adaptation these seem to land better with people.

The output of the session was building common purpose among the teams on what they were trying to achieve, which was enabled by personal connection amongst peers. I got the teams to sign a A3 poster with three principles of intent which I put up in the room. I find public declarations with physical signing of intent is more likely to gain traction than a digital version.

1. Active collaboration is our state of mind
2. We put users at the heart of everything
3. We continually measure, test, and learn

Changing the mindset of senior stakeholders is much harder as it requires a lot of convincing. You have to gain their trust and confidence that what you are doing is making things better. I chose my battles carefully as changing hearts and minds does not happen overnight! I created a hit list of people to focus on with these questions:

1. Who are the hardest people to change?

2. Who would make the most difference to the program if they changed?

3. Who and what are the biggest blockers to change?

Understanding the reasons why they didn't want to change indicates the right course of treatment. I realised their reason was - why would we risk a date on a plan by changing the program way of working mid-flight? They had a case of flawed certainty, a plan with dates and things that needed to be done to hit that date.

Throughout history, humanity has used boundaries and rules to manage uncertainty. In a programme world you can get false certainty by producing rigid scoping documents, plans, and following a prescribed methodology. It's important to have a plan, but it does not stop there, It is more important that the continuous planning occurs with feedback loops of any movement. Rolling-wave planning is probably the best way to drive immediate certainty and providing the flexibility to pivot on things further in the future. I tried a number of things: slide deck presentations, improvement Kanban boards and brown bag lunches. Nothing seemed to work. What I found was that for people to adapt their thinking, I needed to speak their language, come to their level, understand their pressures and demonstrate how and why this would help. I spent time sitting with each person to understand their motivations. It was apparent that there was historic trauma where people had been blamed for missed dates. This was the primary factor for the rigid thinking.

Always remember: mindset shift takes time, and perseverance is key.

For this occasion, what worked best was ensuring I had air cover from senior management as I set to work on high value targets, asking for forgiveness along the way.

I did things that moved the needle forward and tried to bring people along on the journey. You have to agitate people by acting as a solvent to unglue their thinking. This can be achieved by asking the question: why they do things and not stopping asking why until you get a satisfactory answer.

Every day there was a 45-minute stand up where everyone talked about everything without context of the real sprint goals. The scope of sprints had been planned for the next eight months! When functionality was not delivered, they just moved into the next sprint. As a rule of thumb, I find having two sprints or four weeks of work ready for development is more than enough to ensure the team are utilised. The requirements were out of control. We were on version 92 of a spreadsheet with 3,186 requirements and no change history. I managed to get agreement that work could stop for two days while we all got a common understanding of reality. I got all the teams (dev, test, SAs, BAs, PMs) into a room and walked through all the requirements, asking these questions.

- Is the requirement complete and what does it mean?
- Where is it in the lifecycle? Analysis, build, test etc..
- Why is this needed for the MLP (minimal loveable product)?

Just verbalising the requirements in such away unearthed a lot of gaps in terms of scope, delivery, and test.

After the initial cull I moved all the knowledge into Jira and Confluence so we had a single version of the truth. Once I had this, I outlawed any other artefacts, because as soon as anything is extracted, it is out of date. The mantra was: if it's not in Jira or confluence, it does not exist! This does take a while for people to get used to, but it drives the right behaviours where people stop sending you Excel extracts and instead you get a link to a wiki page.

I ran subsequent process-mapping workshops with solution architects and development teams to contextualise the requirements, filling in the gaps between what was being asked for and what was being built. All new requirements were now in Jira as user stories, with business analyst, tech, and test tasks linked to each to track progress. Planning for two sprints ahead and using a centralised tool gave us real-time management reporting and real health metrics for the program. The reporting was objective and based on things that were actually happening, rather than subjective *PowerPoint* status reports. We had a real-time dashboard for every interested party who wanted to see up-the-minute progress of work.

At first the development team were reluctant to show demos of what was being built as they felt it would slow down progress. I believe it was more that they were scared of what we might say, or ask for. Convincing the team to show regular development progress to enable check and challenge was tough! It required three 5,000-mile trips to meet them face to face and see what was going on. With all the collaborative technology in the world nothing beats face-to-face interaction. I spent some time understanding the build and test pipeline, following the paper trail of stories to code to live.

The development team were set up in a hub and spoke model, where the senior developers would digest the requirements, build out component specs and send them out to developers dotted around different offices to build, and then bring it all together with patches to cover the gaps. To fix brittle code you need a sustainable scalable build pipeline where quality is inbuilt. The first thing I did was co-locate the development team and where possible. I reduced the number of branches and put in quality control. Introducing pull requests ensured that senior developers could check the changes, ensuring continuous code quality.

We culled the test scripts, removed non-relevant tests and added new tests that aligned to the real requirements.

The test team automated all the core tests so that they ran every night against the code.

Every morning we had a test report to show if any commits had broken the code, so we could take appropriate action and fix the problem earlier than finding it in user acceptance testing. Remember to focus on measurable outcomes and be mindful that people will blame the process. Rather than measuring against targets, I measured trend against goals. For example, the goal was: deliver quality faster. So I measured the trend of lead time, delivery rate and failure rate. Whenever the trend went in the wrong direction, I was able to understand why and make appropriate action.

If your measurements are complex and reporting is a full time job, then you have probably missed the point! It took a month of fine tuning to see real results; we had managed to turn the ship around and launch the product into live.

The real fun starts when you have real customers on your systems. Things come out of the woodwork. If you have set the team up properly, and they are not burnt-out at launch, then it's just another day at the office post go live. I thoroughly enjoyed the challenge of working in a complex delivery team and I learnt a huge number of lessons along the way.

My key three takeaways are:

1. Your secret weapon is your team. Create a cross functional team and make sure people get to know each other.
    The human connection and the right mindset is key to the success.

2. Connecting the dots. Mini missions to make small changes, review the results, learn and make more small changes.
    Leave everything better than you found it.

3. Things will usually get worse before they get better. Have grit and believe that the change will work and push through.

About Bhavesh Vaghela

Bhavesh is an agile digital craftsman, with experience in strategy, product leadership and digital transformation. He enjoys connecting people and ideas to inspire, innovate and co-create solutions.

An advocate of user experience, human centric design and the intersection between humanity and technology.

Bhavesh is always looking to the next wave of innovation to support customers in their daily lives. He draws on a dynamic range of skills; with over 15 years' experience in senior positions in banking, defence and telecoms.

Bhavesh, originally from Manchester now lives in the Midlands. In his spare time, he enjoys teaching his kids to code, swimming and being inspired by TED talks.

Find out more and connect with Bhavesh on:

www.bhaveshvaghela.com

Deeds Over Words

Angie Main

The underlying theme of this book is one of lessons learned. Throughout it you will hear great examples of how folks have learned from unsuccessful or outdated approaches.

In this chapter I attempt to package my insights as practical action because insight without action, to paraphrase Ken Blanchard, equals squat.

I'll share a couple of the lessons I've learned supporting ways of working programmes over the last 15 years from a non-technical, colleague capability perspective. I hope my own experiences highlight the opportunities you may face and helps shorten your path to better outcomes.

My MO

Action is part of my DNA. I even have deeds not words tattooed on my arm. Throughout my career this bias has helped me in two ways:

- To make useful mistakes - generally achieved through moving forward without thorough preparation or full insight.

- By channeling my curiosity and need for momentum to become a successful early adopter. I try to channel my activator strength into generating momentum, reducing pro-crastination and increasing others confidence to make a start.

Read the following insights with that disclosure in mind.

Manage Yourself, Lead Others

Leadership is a skill that can be taught and learned, in my experience far too little is done to equip leaders (regardless of whether they have direct line responsibility) to understand and adopt new ways of working, let alone enable followers to do the same.

Leadership is about ensuring good outcomes through the application of influence. Too often leaders are expected to move to and deliver effective new ways of working armed with no more than a jazzy new vision statement, a copy of the agile manifesto and set of performance objectives.

Agile and Lean ways of working are both highly people centric - expect limited success unless you invest in leaders. Start by taking a look at existing leadership capability. You will of course have to hire or develop new technical skills but that's easier than developing leadership capability.

Keep front of mind Gallup's insight that says *70% of the variance in employee engagement is directly attributable to manager effectiveness.*

Being keen to just get going, and the resulting failure and time spent retro-fixing, has taught me how important it is to create time to help leaders reflect on their own mind and skill set before embarking on a change initiative.

Start small, equip leaders to understand and manage themselves with a focus on personal effectiveness. Making demands of folks that aren't pretty good at management stuff is a sure way to fail.

Those that can't prioritize, coach, communicate, apply critical thinking and collaborate to an acceptable standard in an existing setting will fail unless helped in practical ways to step into new ways of working.

Optimism alone, I've learned isn't enough.

I've learned the value of making a short, well designed self or 360 degree assessment available and undertaking a skills gap analysis exercise aligned to the key behaviours leaders are expected to demonstrate as part of the change.

Ensure you spend time thinking about what leadership skills and capabilities are important here – ask: *How do we expect folks to lead change?; How do we assess leadership skill?, What's our expectation of leaders and what's our response to gaps?* – ask the organization: *How well developed are coaching and collaboration skills?* and *Show me how you manage and develop both?*

I learned lots from the Dutch company *Verdhoen* while working together supporting a transformation programme at a large UK Food Retailer HQ. The guys took real care in helping leaders understand work-type preference, current capability and placed careful emphasis on having strong foundational skills in place before moving to the public, shiny part of transformation, ensuring leaders could walk before they could run. Together we created training and guidance on topics like *making meetings matter*, virtual working, having quality conversations and collaborating across virtual teams.

- Do not embark on people centric change without a clear idea of the skills and behaviours you expect.

- Avoid excessive analysis, unless you are a very specialised business these are the areas that you should focus on – they also happen to be the skills that enable higher levels of trust and engagement.

- Listening – you'll serve people better when you listen intently.

- Learning – possessing the ability to take up, and act on new information and to facilitate this in others.

- Collaboration – gather diverse views to solve complex issues, together.

- Communication – manage a clear and steady stream of consistent information.

Outcomes Over Methodology

A typical pivot has been the need to help organizations move from talking less about methodology and more about outcome. Specifically stepping back from an upper case narrative i.e., one that focuses on doing or becoming *Agile* or *Lean*. Both are journeys, not destinations.

In an effort to create cut through and enthusiasm, it's really tempting to try and jazz up your change programme, marketing colleagues with eye-catching language.

Don't, instead use simple language to talk about outcomes i.e., what you can expect to see, hear and feel when we're getting this right and, most importantly how you can contribute.

It's vital that you make it as easy as possible for folks to understand the ask, translate operational into functional language and cover both the what and how of new ways of working.

Spend time to help leaders describe the change confidently, what does it mean for them? How will they and their team contribute to change? How will progress be seen and measured.

Try and reduce hesitancy and help leaders manage uncertainty.

One of most satisfying contributions I've made was as part of a long-lived large retail banking transformation, translating a hefty strategic plan with multiple aims and pages of things to be changed into two call to actions.

Simply stating we want to get really good at two things, *Continuous Improvement* and *Productive Collaboration* – *we need you to contribute to those two outcomes please.*

There is an undisputed issue with poor employee engagement globally as organisations have failed to keep up with the changing nature of work. Typically less than 30% of your workforce is likely to be very engaged in the work it does – most people are trying to get through the day with the least hassle and clearest direction as possible.

Make it easy to understand what you want from folk and report on signs of progress often, don't oversell the benefits or declare victory too soon.

In 1995, John Kotter published his seminal article on why transformation fails - he outlined 8 reasons that are as pertinent today as then. Error number 4/8 is under *communicating the vision*. I believe Kotter meant falling short on both the quality and cadence of communication, inconsistent and sporadic news on expectation and progress stymies engagement.

I'll offer another important pivot to this point; move from thinking about broadcast communication (getting information out) to dialogue (getting through).

Shift your focus from traditional comms planning to an approach that's about driving dialogue. Pay attention to facilitation and conflict management skills – true dialogue is multi directional and facetted (and can get untidy). Ensure you have a response strategy and hand-hold if necessary senior folks who worry about retaining control.

Wonky Works

"Think curation, not creation" Rachel Miller, all things IC

I stumbled on my next pivot due to the common issue of lack of resource allocated to colleague engagement activity and my general aversion to overly fastidious comms planning. I've been working to this principle for close to a decade, my most successful colleague communication programmes have been the ones where I've produced and facilitated quick turnaround wonky comms whether that's on-behalf of an audience of 14,000 or 800.

Wonky comms sums up an approach that encourages employee voice and multi directional dialogue; it grasps new channels and accepts comms activity that is good enough over perfect. Comms (not the underlying message) are often quirky and designed to be short-lived. Remember you're striving for outcome over methodology.

Your audience does not value ghost written memos, polished talking head-style films, branded stress ball giveaways and staged back to the floor activity – all part of a traditional campaign.

Your audience is seeking and listening to new sources of information and demanding they too be heard. *The Edelmann Trust Barometer* (2018) report reiterates the importance of peer-to-peer communication in a world where trust has stagnated and makes a case for CEO as advocates of truth counteracting a climate of disinformation.

Look to leverage a tone of voice that's authoritative and authentic when considering your comms approach.

Here are a few things that work:

- **Nudges** – whether that's twitter, short 30 sec low-fi films, Yammer posts or use of imagery to report progress – keep up your cadence and don't rely on email.

- **Keep it visual** – I always include high levels of visual activity in any people plan. Whether that's a paper tablecloth to doodle on, sessions to help people learn to draw/make flip charts more interesting, lightning talks over chalk and talk or animated video over talking head. Don't ignore print items.

- **Merchandise** - protect the oceans, do not buy stress balls or horrid branded plastic giveaways. If you insist on a giveaway, keep it useful. Pens and notepads work.

- **Unleash colleague creativity** – use real colleague faces *and* voiceovers, record items in folk's primary language and subtitle if needed. Use platforms that encourage folks to upload and share stories of success. Help your brand police to relax a little, create brand artifacts that colleagues can easily replicate or use.

- **Silly Stuff** – I'm proud of the now infamous line of paper underwear I strung end to end in a *innovation lab* with the functions current (long line of impediments) written on in marker. *Impediments are pants,* silly and provocative, but boy did it garner traction.

- **Info graphic and Sketch note** – time and again *PowerPoint* is perpetuated due to lack of creative confidence – find a few folks who can doodle and train sketchnoting – I've seen 20-page decks distilled to one page very effectively.

- **Experiential** – pop up cardboard fireplaces and rugs for story telling sessions.

Leading Hippos and Horses to Water

This final section is simply about pivoting effort from push to pull. I've learned it's much easier and more sustainable to invite, not drag hippos (the power holders) and horses (the do-oers) to water.

My most recent work has been supporting change in large Financial Services organizations, ones that are complex and diverse. The last two years has reminded me that folks will not budge and engage with change until they are ready, and the exact moment of readiness is hard to predict. I've learned to reject the promise of large scale, generic adoption of scaling frameworks over smaller pockets of context sensitive (situational) change. Again focusing on outcome over methodology.

Old Model – change thinking to change behavior
New Model – change behavior to change thinking

Small can be good, smaller sized teams dealing with smaller investment, reduced risk and appropriately sized business outcomes can grease the tracks of change and help provide stories of experimentation and progress.

Plenty of folks have referenced the Kubler-Ross curve when discussing the emotional passage to change, it's a powerful model that articulated the typical stages of grief and is a useful lens when laid on top of work-based change. This model encourages folks to meet people where they are on the curve and respond appropriately. I recommend taking a look at Kubler-Ross.

I've turned my intention instead to John Shook's work who Jon Smart , *Barclays Head of Ways of Working,* introduced me to. I like Shook's action bias; Shook was *Toyota's* first American *kacho* (manager) in Japan. Shook proposes we replace a way of thinking that leverages and relies on culture shift to change behaviors and replace with a focus on changing behaviors first – pivot your attention to action over intent.

His model shows how we tend to try to shift culture first and treat action *what we do* as an outcome – he suggests we invert that, *do stuff* and let culture take hint and follow.

Both Shook and Kubler-Ross I think help me see the sense in (John Smart's words) big through small.

In summary, I restate my bias and suggest a course of action that's about deeds over words. Good luck.

About Angie Main

Angie Main, Activator – Intellection – Strategic – Learner – Relator, works in the areas of organizational development and employee engagement, she specializes in developing and delivering creative yet practical programs to help folks engage with new ways of working. Angie has an eclectic skill set which helps her contribute across boundaries. Angie spent 17 years at a senior leader level within FS before moving to interim and consultancy work across a range of sectors.

Angie advocates Servant Leadership, has two rescue dogs, a passion for lighthouses and the Northumberland coast where she lives.

https://www.linkedin.com/in/angie-main-22265620/

Pivoting The Agile Hero
To An All-Stars Agile Team

Karan Jain

Agile Leadership

Ever heard of an *agile hero*? We all know one: The member of the agile team who takes it upon themselves to save the day, rescue the project, ensures the sprint target is hit. The goal has to be met, do or die! Culturally, the hero behaviour is regularly rewarded in various forms, this also creates an immense people and cultural issues for the organisation – and we, as leaders are all guilty of promoting it. The question is how do you pivot the agile hero to an all-stars agile team?

Agile is built on founding principles of people and culture, we can implement the best practices and tools, but if the team and individuals do not embrace right behaviours, the agile journey is most likely not making the most of it. As leaders, we are in the business of people and should recognise these anti-patterns, use advice listed here to maximise the opportunity.

Spotting behaviours and anti-patterns that can impact your journey is an essential first step. Let's evaluate Jo's case, with a filter of culture, agile delivery and leadership.

Jo was one of the best development leads on a large, multi-million, multiyear equities digital transformation program, the team had circa 300 staff, aiming to meet a regulatory deadline and at the same time to increase the digital offering for the customer base.

Commercially, there was an enormous time to market urgency between two leading products in the market (by *Company X* and *Company B*), aiming broadly at the same objective. Meeting the regulatory deadline timely meant that you also had the opportunity to increase your wallet share by targeting competitor's customers. The arms race was on, and both projects chose to adopt agile as their preferred method of delivery.

To everyone's surprise, within twelve months of the three-year program, *Company B* was able to ship the MVP product and starting to attract interest from competition's customers, by the eighteen-month mark, *Company B* had acquired additional twenty percent wallet share. If the scope was same, delivery was same; the budgets were similar, and let's assume both teams were talented– so what was the differential?

Company B went to the market and collected market feedback and fed it back into their delivery cycle as a matter of priority. Whereas, *Company X* adopted the agile approach, built the product but didn't ship it till it was finished.

Back to Jo, she was an excellent technologist; she had been with the organisation for reasonable tenure; she knew the undocumented architecture, her rooted knowledge of the product made her a key person. The teams were set up in guilds and tribes (look at *Spotify* model). Jo's curse of knowledge slowed her output, which caused her frustration and she saw teaching others as a distraction.

A common theme for Jo was to get the work over the line; she mostly went for team exhaustion by pushing the team hard and setting the anti-pattern as a standard, rather than the completion of the goal as a team at a sustainable pace. However, Jo gave her very best and was very committed to the organisation's purpose. The best part of her day was saving the day – multiple times a day if she could – it was a high for her. She was worshipped by managers alike and imagined her team thought of her as a superhero. The real secret was that not only did she regularly take on the hero role, but she also loved it.

Culturally, we often put heroes on a pedestal, and we protect, worship and treat very delicately knowing that if they were to leave, the entire department might collapse. Almost nobody considers that the hero is a big impediment to the organisation, risk and a situation to avoid.

In an agile team, these behaviours undermine the spirit of self-organisation for the team. Jo's team felt that she was seen as a hero, and started accepting her estimates, stopped challenging her design challenges and bringing collaboration to a halt. The level of the hero becomes its own ceiling for the team. We observe similar patterns where a hero can impose an unhealthy pressure on delivery, as well as the team, can feel obliged to long hours as that is worshipped culturally.

The hero could also, unknowingly chase the team away as the hero tends to achieve a position that is unquestionable, either people accept that or people walk away. This is mostly the reactive behaviour choice of the team, and the people walking away are the people you want to keep for increased collaboration and springing new and better ways of working.

Typical heroic behaviour can be repeated weekend work, particular system knowledge, last minute deliveries, and repeat offenders of saving the day, why is this happening? Leaders should explore what is driving this behaviour. Does it make them feel a more valued member of the team or to be seen as the star member? Or is it to compensate their inability to add value relative to others, or could it even be that they are unclear on their role?

The key is to identify the drivers and where the sense of achievement is driven from, by unlocking and helping them discover their passion.

Once identified– it is much easier to pivot them into outstand-ing contributors and influencers. You can ensure this is part of the periodic catch ups and you create an environment to pause and reflect.

A potential avenue to break the pattern is ensuring during team sessions; e.g. the team estimates tasks for a sprint together before they are assigned to people, that encourages open discussion and debate on how long something will take. Ensure it is a safe environment; others are not underquoting in fear of the hero or agreeing with the estimates provided by them. Simple questioning techniques assist with the understanding of how the quote is built and increases the knowledge as a team.

Jo's manager viewed her as a life saver, keeping the delivery on track at the cost of personal sacrifice, commitment; she was highly reliable and always going the extra mile. But, her manager started to note emerging anti-patterns and observed the impacts on the team. Such as bottle necks, quality issues, increasingly longer hours and team morale issues. It was also worrying that she might not be able to keep the same pace, and lack of alternatives for when she is not around.

Over a period, the heroic behaviours tend to beat their personal best, which has its limits and can result in increased reliance on the hero.

Most of us are always racing against the clock with competing priorities, in a cheaper faster better environment and sometimes it is easier to call on heroes and create situations that lead to the creation of the hero. The first step to prevent a hero from being found to prepare or adjust the environment of the project or team to remove the characteristics which can make heroes thrive. After they are created, it becomes costly and disruptive to dismantle.

Permitting individual work inside a team or creating silos by design increases the chances of heroes to be born for specific parts of the ecosystem. Allow a more collaborative workflow by fostering critical decisions from the team and not an individual. Techniques such as 'pairing' to share knowledge and skills to remove that individuality, pairing can be applied to any function within a team.

Your Role As A Leader Is Hard

It is sometimes hard not to cry out for a hero, especially in a moment of crisis. Creating heroes doesn't change the individual. Usually, they return to ordinary work after, in search of the next heroic moment – disheartened if it doesn't present itself. Similarly, we have all seen favouritism towards others; the after taste is a varying degree of disengagement or shortened motivation. Having even just a few people in hero positions can be a sign of bad leadership. Everybody in the organisation is vital and should be positioned as part of the true value chain.

Leaders should foster environments where the team as a whole is valued and appreciated. It is not to say that we shouldn't acknowledge individual efforts. After a job well done and recognising the team, if you feel someone deserves more, tell them in person. It will be valued more by the individual. The difference here is not to nominate the same individual repeatedly in a forum. To pivot the heroic behaviour to the broader group, explore the sentiment that drives that behaviour for the individual.

As leaders, our role is to help our teams to pause and reflect and look forward. This may mean, we have a short-term loss or take a hit on delivery, but it is for a long-term gain that results in an amplified group that works well together. Explaining this to the customer can be a challenge, but that is why you are the leader.

It is also essential that leaders explore the cause and impact with the individual and they see the situation in a more prominent perspective, examining how they can channel the same motivation to bring a sizeable impact.

One possibility is that they can achieve the same level of satisfaction by teaching skills or educating others as part of the team and remain to be the respected SME.

Help the individual with prioritising work at the juncture of passion and dedication. With the information in hand, you are better equipped to identify that sweet spot where their passion and contribution to the team overlaps. Also, creating room for others to grow with that challenge and allowing the hero to become a leader.

If you find yourself in this situation, I recommend replacing the demand for heroism and sacrifice to setting a goal of sustainable goals. As a result, the team becomes confident in their abilities without the hero of the team. You could assign the very task to someone else, it is vital that it is done collaboratively and not as a directive. Equally important, for the hero, is that you replace it with something that meets their passion and they can continue to add value, hopefully at a magnified scale. This is not a technical task; your empathy plays a big part in this.

We also have some off-the-shelf agile techniques and principles at our disposal, ability to implement simple tweaks can enhance the performance as well as break the anti-patterns. Take sprint planning – restrict the work that is done in the current *sprint* discourages sudden changes of priority, which can trigger heroic behaviours. Most things can wait till next sprint. Monitor, if individuals always gravitate towards the same task – another sign of heroic anti-pattern. Daily stand-ups and regular customer interactions are your prime time opportunities to spot the heroes.

Agile delivery is a team sport.

The traditional image of heroism does not fit all-stars agile team. A leader should be equipped to spot both a culture of hero worship and individuals who engage in self-sacrificial behaviour at the cost of long-term sustainability. As simple as it may sound, acknowledging the behaviour of the hero and the leader can be a simple step. Once the passion and the driver behind the behaviour have been identified, it is possible to channel this positively for a significant impact on a team.

Are you ready to pivot your agile hero to the all-star agile team?

About Karan Jain

Karan Jain is a business-oriented technology executive, who is driven by solving complex business problems. Being agile since 2002, and specialist in the Financial Services sector. Karan has a unique perspective on the common challenges faced by the industry and the urgent need to be agile. Karan is very passionate about coaching and training in agile, *Kanban*, *SAFe* and developed his signature modular agile training course set a few years ago, keeping time poor agile executives in mind. He is an energetic leader, coach and mentor to sizeable teams.

His keen ability to identify business drivers, address deep-rooted issues and work with leadership teams within a large organisation has originated from his hands-on experience of not only implementing methodologies but also being in delivery and operation roles within Financial Services organisations.

Karan has been previously published a book on 24/7 software development and enjoys speaking at a variety of events, delivering lectures in universities on the topics of lean, agile and disruptive business models.

Karan also remains an active member of the start-up community as co-founder, investor and advisor.

karanjainonline.com

Daring Conversations:
Harnessing The Agility of Individuals and Interactions

Andrew Kidd

I find it helpful to think of an organisation as being the symbiotic relationship between two systems: a social system (individuals and their interactions); and a technical system (the processes and tools supporting and enhancing the social system). Their interaction is how work gets done, which either sustains the organisation's purpose, or the organisation perishes. The technical system of a modern enterprise often comprises of a significant amount of software, customised for its own specific needs.

If the organisational goal is to meet the needs of it's market, it follows then that it must adapt the software of its operations and service offerings more rapidly that its competitors, in order to give sustain a competitive advantage. This creates a demand for any technologies that support this goal. Such technologies can be deployed to either (or both) the technical and social systems, and can come in the form of tools, techniques and practices for thinking, doing and being together.

The *Agile Manifesto* is an example of such a technology. It comprises of four values and 12 principles which, when combined together, create an emergent strategy that guides the organisation to becoming more effective and responsive to change. Agile coaches are, therefore, change agents that specialise in the application of this emergent strategy, supporting the process and behavioural changes needed to adapt to this way of working.

It's fair to say then, that an important measure of an organisation's adaptive and responsive effectiveness (referred to as agility) is the combined output of the individuals and interactions (social system) with processes and tools (technical system). And we see an acknowledgement of this interdependence baked into the first value of the manifesto, together with an emphasis on the word *over* - a cautionary recognition that a fool with a tool is still a fool.

So Why Then Do We Focus On Process?

I see novice agile coaches, change sponsors and clients making a common mistake, which is being unable to focus on anything but the tools and processes of Agile. As far as I can tell, this is due to three main reasons.

The first is due to a cognitive phenomena (the ironic process theory - also known as the white bear problem). To illustrate this, try the following challenge - do not think of a pink elephant. Did you? Don't worry, it's entirely normal behaviour since as the theory predicts, when we try to suppress certain thoughts, we actually make them more likely to surface. Therefore, being asked not to focus on process and tools is more likely to bias us into doing just that.

The second reason supports the first, and is entirely understandable, since 81% of Agile methods and practices are in fact process focussed. It was Deming that said, "If you can't describe what you are doing as a process, you don't know what you're doing." So even competent reasoning, let alone *Agile* practices, are biasing outcomes. But it's the final reason I want to speak to, which can be illustrated in this short story.

The great Sufi master Mullah Nasruddin was on his hands and knees searching for something under a streetlamp. A man saw him and asked, "What are you looking for?"

"My house key," Nasruddin replied. "I lost it."

The man joined him in looking for the key, and after a period of fruitless searching, the man asked, "Are you sure you lost it around here?"

Nasruddin replied, "Oh, I didn't lose it around here. I lost it over there, in that alley."

"Then why," the man asked, "are you looking for it over here?"

"Because," Nasruddin said, "The light is so much better over here."

Just like Nasruddin, the agile manifesto predicts that we've a tendency to look in the wrong place (technical system) and suggests that greater agility can be had by focussing on the social system (individuals and their interactions).

Why then, despite the guidance to the contrary, do we look in the wrong place? In my experience, there are three main causes of this: challenges in the social system are harder to spot; they are harder to work with; and often people don't know how resolve them. Worse still, the resulting frustration creates a negative feedback loop that moves the change focus back onto the process and tools, as we revert to facing and solving problems we feel capable of tackling and have an impact on, when under pressure to deliver something, or anything delivered under pressure.

Should Have Gone To Specsavers

Human beings look at their reality through lenses - their definitions of things. If the lens through which I'm viewing reality is affecting the reality itself in a way that is not congruent with my commitment, then instead of trying to change the reality, maybe I should change my definition? One of the jobs of a coach is to make those lenses apparent, so clients have choice - is this lens working for them, or not?

I've found that the first step towards working with a lens is to accept that I have one, and then understand where I'm pointing it. Try this now before reading on. Go to *https://youtu.be/ Ahg6qcgoay4* and take the awareness test.

What was that like for you? Are you aware of your lenses? What is it that you're currently not noticing? Are your lenses serving you and your customers? If they're not, what would?

The effect you've just observed is called sustained in-attentional blindness and is the work of cognitive psychologist Daniel Simons. Now that you have a handle on one lens, let's see if I can help you focus it on the challenges facing the social system.

The Challenges Of Collaboration

The advantages of collaborative practices over communication or coordination with hand-offs, are clear. However, such working practices introduce a level of trans-parency and accountability that can be uncomfortable for some people. The quality and turnaround time of our work becomes, quite literally, in plain sight of our teammates. This is daunting to the uninitiated or introverted.

Another challenge comes from managing inevitable conflict - both intra-personal and interpersonal. The stakes are high as many change implementations occur on live projects, with little rehearsal in simulations or practice environments. The rapid and iterative nature of Agile projects can often create feelings that might be associated with being asked to reconfigure a biplane into a jet airliner, once it's left the ground, and whilst travelling on it! And with our profession-al reputations at risk in such ventures, perhaps this is why workplace stress and disengagement is now a sizeable global problem. These factors are further compounded with face-to-face interactions increasing the likelihood of inter-personal conflict in these highly collaborative *Agile* activities.

Then there's the clash of management philosophies. Organisations with a history of focussing on worker efficiency (or utilisation) struggle to accept that 100% worker efficiency reduces flow efficiency. Years of investment in optimising for specialisation creates structures, such as performance related incentives, and negative consequences for project budget under-utilisation.

By contrast, the Agile focus on flow efficiency appears counterintuitive, possibly even counter-cultural, despite the benefits being well documented and understood.

Finally, there may be little recognition in the organisational culture for the value of collaboration itself, with many confusing collaboration with communication and coordination.

In a recent survey when asked "What was the biggest challenge to adopting and scaling agile?", 63% of the respondents cited *company philosophy* or *culture at odds with core agile values*, and 47% cited *lack of experience with Agile methods* as their reason.

Copyright Walt Kelly used with kind permission from Fantagraphics (USA).

A breakfast rap

What does this look like in practice? During a coaching engagement with a financial services client, I was asked to facilitate the project initiation between a product team, and a build team based in India, who were beaming in live via video-conferencing kit. My role was to support the rapid creation of a collaborative team culture, to enable everyone to deliver at pace.

I started by eliciting the project timeline from the product owner, and drew it on the whiteboard. The project, valued at around £1.1M, had been planned in three phases; three months for the requirements phase, producing a product backlog (done); a 6 months build phase; and an 18 month run phase, for the benefits realisation. I started to get an odd feeling in my stomach and did a stocktake of the situation:

- the backlog was non-negotiable

- this had been done without any engineering input

- the project plan had no allowances for testing any of the leap-of-faith assumptions in the business case

- this group had never worked together before

- this was their first exposure to delivery using an Agile method

- the project was to credit the business unit in meeting externally set targets for investment spend delivered using an *Agile* method

- and everyone was (so far) being terribly polite and nice to each other, in a culture that penalised deviation from predicted budget burn-down, and where everyone's year-end bonuses were linked to project performance

- A further question unveiled that I was expected to use my *Agile* wizardry to squeeze down the six months build time, which I was told was the key factor in the project's success.

Suddenly the room felt like a darkened gunpowder store, and I'd just lit a match to see where I was.

- *Boom!* This is how strategies are eaten for breakfast. (Drops mic).

Old light through new windows

So, what can we do to improve the efficacy coaching engagements, and keep coaches safe? The results of my coaching experiences has shown me that when my clients and I have the same view of the organisation's social system, shift happens! Whilst this sounds simple, it's far from simplistic, as many of you already know.

Every coach knows that questions are the tools of their trade, and these can be grouped and crafted into elegant use in client conversations. At this point, both coach and client can be sure that a shared perspective has been established. I have found that a cycle of four focussed conversations generates an awareness of the social system landscape that we're trying to traverse. Even not knowing or being able to answer a question yields an insight which is of value.

In the diagram below, you'll see the four conversations arranged into a framework that I call *Daring Conversations*.

Each conversation is a specific lens onto the social system, and by engaging with it, a detailed and shared view can emerge. By shared I mean between coach and client, if in an executive coaching context, or between coach and team members if in a team coaching context. In the latter case, there is enormous value to be had by team members hearing each other engage with the questions, even if no immediate answers emerge or can be agreed on. This will, and should, test the coach's facilitation skills, and the cohesion of the team culture. Better to do this now than later when under the pressure of deadlines to deliver.

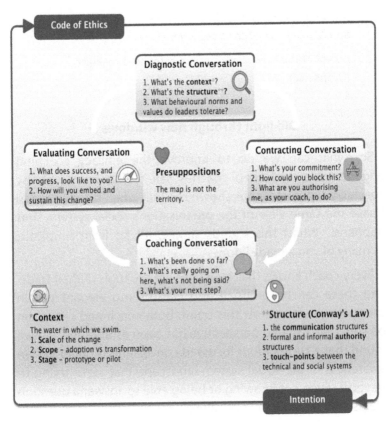

daringfutures.com/DaringConversations

It's important to note that the efficacy of *Daring Conversations* is entirely dependent upon the degree of psychological safety that can be created.

It's for this reason that the four conversations are bounded by the code of ethics and intention. The engagement starts with an agreement between all parties as to the ethical standards that we're going to share, as well as the intentions for the engagement. With these explicitly agreed, the outer frame is created, within which we can operate safely (both psychologically and commercially), and authentically.

If the frame is broken, stop, and renegotiate. Do not proceed unless it's safe to do so. Remember, it's daring, not reckless.

"Ethics is how we behave when we decide we belong together."
Brother David Steindl-Rast

With expectations being managed, we can engage in the cycle of conversations that form the four lenses. The natural flow is diagnostic (understand the work), contracting (agree the work), coaching (support the work), and evaluating (assess the work). However, you could start wherever makes sense in your particular circumstances. The cycle can be iterated as many times as needed, and indeed, I've known cycles span from a matter of minutes to several months. This process should feel quite natural to most Agile coaches, who will be used to the iterative nature of their work. The value I'm hoping to add here is to illustrate how their existing talents can be repurposed to enhance their traction in tackling the challenges and supporting change in the social system.

I hope this is useful, and wish you every success (and safety) in your own daring futures.

About Andrew Kidd

Andrew is the Chief Learning Officer for the UK based Daring Futures (a boutique coaching consultancy), where he supports clients in the creation and commercialisation of elegant solutions to sophisticated problems.

A keen modeller, Andrew has been fascinated with simulating real-life problems through the metaphors of software programming languages since the early 80's.

A degree in engineering design and manufacture gave Andrew a disciplined foundation for a career in the practical application of technology in delivering solutions in complex and rapidly changing environments. Clients include: *Barclaycard, Deutsche Bank, HSBC Bank, DWP, HMRC, Cabinet Office, Metropolitan Police, The Royal Navy, Estée Lauder*, and *Pfizer*.

With certifications including *Scrum Product Owner*, and *ICF Professional Certified Coach (PCC)*, Andrew is qualified in coaching both the technical and social systems of an organisation. And as a serial entrepreneur himself, Andrew recognises the unique challenges facing start-up founders and teams, business owners, as well as product and service managers.

Andrew works with teams and individuals in the development and execution of strategy, as well as business and operating model design.

Currently living in the UK, Andrew is married with five children, who all enjoy exploring the delights of the UK's inland waterways on narrowboats.

https://www.linkedin.com/in/coachkidd/

A New Hope

David Smith

We value individuals and interactions over processes and tools. It sounds like a statement of the obvious. Why wouldn't we?

The reality can be different, however as we become immersed in corporate governance structures and bureaucratic culture. Human interaction is easily lost as the boundaries defined by departments and job descriptions, and the limitations imposed by hierarchy and role status take over. The customer and their product, as well as how we work as a team, can become secondary or worse.

Personal experience has taught me two key lessons relating to these interactions. Write less, talk more.

- Do not rely on documents and emails to communicate with people. A document that is read by five different people will most likely have five different interpretations.

- Talk regularly with your customers to get their feedback and pass this on to the people building your product.

- Talk, face to face, regularly (daily) with the people who are building your product.

- Repeat the above until you have built something that you are proud to present to your customers.

I first learned about the value of individuals and interactions over processes and tools through a combination of intuition and a chance meeting with a great developer.

The Process

For many years I worked as a product manager in a FTSE 100 media and technology company where I oversaw the launch of several new products. These were used in banks across their front, middle and back office functions. After a few launches I was well-versed in the process you were expected to follow, but I had also learned enough to recognise a pattern that kept repeating itself. You may not know the company, but you would probably recognise the process which followed a linear, *stage gate* approach to product delivery that looked something like this.

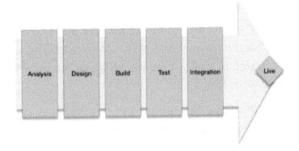

As a rule, the process start-ed well. My role was to understand customer requirements. These early days were exciting as this was the time for lots of new ideas and creative thinking. I enjoyed this phase as it gave me the opportunity to spend time with my customers and the account teams that supported them.

I would work hard to take the ideas gathered through these conversations and build them into an image of a product. I would come up with lots of new features that would be invaluable for my customers.

Over time this would build into a functional specification, an essential requirement of the process, and its creation was a key milestone.

As the product gained shape other elements of the process would kick in. One would come in the form of a project manager. In line with the process, it was the project manager who would introduce me to the *iron triangle* or *project management triangle*. Many will be familiar with it but for those who are not, it looks like this;

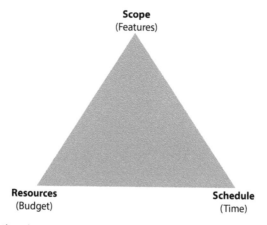

Scope
(Features)

Resources
(Budget)

Schedule
(Time)

So, whilst there were lots of ideas, we were now constrained by the fact that a senior executive had predetermined our schedule by selecting an (apparently) arbitrary date in the future when the product would need to be delivered, say in 12 months time.

Then more resources (people) would get allocated, based on the process. This became another implicit constraint on our capacity to deliver

For more complex products, I would be allocated the support of business analysts to help prepare my functional specification. On one occasion I was consulting on a programme where there were no less than 16 business analysts working to produce a single functional specification. Mind boggling!

I would also be introduced to a development team, usually in a different location to me and often spread across one or more countries. They were always part of a different department within the organisation and seen as distinct from the *business* and its dealings with the customers.

All of these new factors would be combined with the help of the project manager to produce a project plan looking something like this:

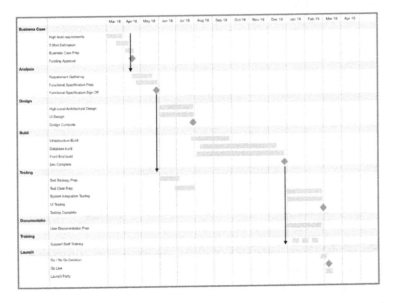

At this point I was advised that my long and exciting list of ideas was going to need to be reviewed, refined and ultimately greatly shortened. In spite of all this my vision for my product and the energy required to deliver it remained largely intact.

To agree the scope of the first release I would need to talk with the development team. In the interests of observing the hierarchy I would not speak to junior developers and would work only with the technical leads to agree the release scope.

After numerous discussions with these technical leads, I would finally get to the point where I could sign off a functional specification document for the release. And maybe if I was lucky, my manager would sign it off too. And maybe if I was really lucky, their manager too. This was a significant event. A milestone in the plan had been reached. With any luck we were on target.

The process then dictated that I should hand over the functional specification to the development team. At that point, for me at least, things would go quiet. I might have occasional calls with a technical lead,

Me: "How's it going?"

Tech Lead: "All fine, we've got a couple of challenges, but we'll work them out."

...but mostly it was quiet for me ... until testing began.

Reality Bites

At this point things would change again. I'd be working at my desk and I'd receive a tap on my shoulder from the project manager, or maybe the testing manager.

PM: "Errr, Dave, can we have a word?",

Me: "Yep. No problem."

PM: "Actually, it's a bit delicate. Can we go into a room?"

Me: "Ah. OK"

PM: "Errr. You are not going to like this. We've completed ten days of testing ... and so far we've discovered 78 defects ... and 39 of those are critical ... we can't go live with them."

This was a turning point. From then on my role as product manager would become a series of decisions where I needed to make a choice between compromising on quality and accepting defects in my product, or reducing the scope.

I was hampered further by the fact that changes to scope often required a *Change Request*. This meant more documents to be prepared, reviewed and signed off and in turn, further scope reductions/delays.

Whilst I may have thought that these processes were cumbersome at the time, I can still feel the scars of the process in an organisation I was working with years many later. Here the standard SLA on any *Change Request* was six weeks. To be clear, this was not to deliver the change itself, rather to complete the analysis that would reveal the effort required to deliver the new feature, fix the defect or even remove an item of scope.

Back to my stage gate release process, and by now I was intensely frustrated. At the point that testing began the risks and unknowns that we had been unwittingly building up would be revealed. The workload and stress levels would soar and they would reach their crescendo at the point where the product finally launched.

Looking back at the *iron triangle* that I had been introduced to by my project manager, this is where we would usually find ourselves;

- The product launch would be delayed by a week, maybe two, maybe more.

- The project would run over budget. After all we had run beyond schedule and potentially had to employ contract *resource* to help us deliver.

- We would not deliver all of the scope that we had agreed in the original functional specification document.

I was reminded of this feeling several years later, when working with a client. Having dropped by the desk of a product manager I had just been brought in to help, I recognised the panicked disbelief on his face when he told me the development lead had informed him that actually they would need to scale back the scope of the demo dramatically for the long planned showcase meeting next week.

They been slowed down by a series of issues that had arisen during testing and integration. It sent a little, shivery memory down my spine.

A Competitive Threat

I was growing weary of repeating the same energy sapping process when a new opportunity presented itself. I was asked to take over a product for a major strategic initiative which had been put in place to combat a competitive threat.

Market pressures meant that our clients were looking to reduce their costs and a key way for them to do this was to reduce the number of data vendor terminals being used in their trading rooms. One competitor had an instant messaging product built into their terminal which was proving to be a key differentiator and was causing vast numbers of our customers to select their terminals instead of ours.

This was going to impact our premium product which brought in about $1 billion annually. In short, senior management were extremely worried.

As a product manager in the team building our response we were tasked with creating our own messaging service. As the project went on I recognised that the process described above had started again and the familiar, unproductive pattern was beginning to emerge. We were set for another round of stress, unsustainable workloads and an unsatisfactory outcome for our customers. Having recognised the pattern and struggling with how we could break it, I was complaining about the process over a drink one evening.

A New Individual

A developer (we'll call him Mike) who was also in the bar told me that he would be able to build a messaging product like the one I was building with my team. What's more, he said he could build me something in a week. Impossible. I had a team who had been toiling with this problem for weeks and at the time had nothing, literally nothing, to show me.

I was sceptical but on Mike's insistence I agreed to go and see him and his colleague (we'll call him Jeff) a week later. A week passed and we met up and Mike took my laptop, fiddled around with it and after a few minutes handed it back to me.

Then, I received my first instant message. Admittedly it was from Mike who was sitting right next to me at the time, nonetheless it worked. The messaging application was not pretty by any means. But it worked. After one week I could use something that actually worked.

I discussed a few ideas with Mike and requested a couple of changes. Mike said to leave it with him and come back in a couple of days, which I did, and when I went to see him, there were the changes I had asked for.

This was brilliant!

Having gained more experience since this time and having worked with developers who routinely make changes in a day or half a day, or even right in front of me, it seems extraordinary that I was so impressed by this. At the time, however the stage gate process had caused me to be so remote from my development team that I had totally lost touch with how my team worked and what they were capable of.

Better Interactions

This process of iterative improvement continued for a few weeks. I was able to take the requirements that I had picked up from spending time on the trading floors of my customers and ask Mike and Jeff to work on them. As I built up my relationship with the customers I could discuss more ideas with them and then talk these through with Mike and Jeff who would work on the solutions we agreed.

Furthermore, since I always had a working version of the product on my laptop I was able to show it to the account teams as well as my senior management for their review and input on a regular basis. We would have conversations about how the product was evolving and discuss ideas for improvements which I could take back to Mike and Jeff. I did not need to schedule infrequent, formal review sessions which never generated the rich feedback these informal conversations did.

I have seen this work in many organisations since this first experience. It is almost always better to have these conversations face to face but they can work between different locations. Frequently part of my role is to help bridge the gap (be it cultural, organisational or physical) between the business and the delivery team. This is best done through conversation.

We continued to work like this over the coming months where I would go and see Mike and Jeff, they would show me the latest changes and I would comment and make additional requests for new features, modify work that had been completed or remove features that just did not work out as I had expected them to.

Ultimately we arrived at product launch. I am not going to say it was stress-free, or that we did not work extremely hard, but it all felt much more worthwhile when we went to market with a product we genuinely believed our customers wanted.

Reflections

Reflecting on the process and the Gantt Chart that I described earlier there were a couple of key lessons I learned: *Write Less* and *Talk More*.

Write Less

- Documents, be they functional specs, design documents or emails do not lead to a common understanding. A single document will have as many interpretations as it has readers. Jeff Patton uses a simple diagram to illustrate this.

I'm glad we all agree

Conversation is the key. In my conversations with Mike and Jeff, I am not sure I referenced the functional specification I had so diligently prepared at the beginning of the project but relied on these conversations and the product itself to explain my requirements and build out the service into something that fitted our customers' needs.

Talk More

- Talk more with your customers. Spend time with them and listen carefully to understand their needs.

- Talk more with your development team, daily if possible. Voice your customer needs and work with them, face to face, to agree a way of delivering a product that you will be proud of.

- Talk more with your leadership. Seek their views, gather their feedback and respond to it, even if you don't include it all in your product.

- Don't allow the process to dictate when you can talk. Don't wait for formal events and sign offs to get feedback. Knock on doors and talk to people about what you are working on.

My Project Manager may not have recognised it, or signed it off, but we were still completing all of the activities outlined in the project plan, just on a much shorter timeframe. We incorporated changes based on customer input that did not require a series of documents coupled to a complex *Change Request* process.

I had ignored a lot of the formal *stage gate* process however since many of the account teams and my senior management had been engaged in the development throughout the process, I had strong support for the service that we had built. This helped me circumnavigate all but the most critical parts of the process. After all they had a stake in the work. They were engaged and had bought into the product already and believed it would succeed in the market.

Post Script

The messaging product we built together was released into the financial services sector and registered over 100,000 users within one year of launch. It is still in use today a little over 15 years later and is integrated into the flagship product of the company. It boasts over 300,000 users across 180 countries. It remains one of my proudest professional achievements.

At the time I was totally unaware of formal Agile frameworks such as Scrum or XP and the *Agile Manifesto* had only just been written. It certainly had not made its way into my consciousness. I was simply doing what seemed sensible to me and that remains as true today as it was then.

I am confident that the company had adopted the *stage gate* process that I had seen fail so often with good intentions, however it did not factor in the human element of delivery that is fundamental to teams working well together. We succeeded once we shifted the emphasis away from the process and focussed on how we as individuals could interact to deliver the best possible product for our customers.

About David Smith

David Smith has been working in IT for over 20 years. David is passionate about helping companies to focus on making their customers' lives better as well as making organisations into the types of places where people want to go to enjoy their jobs. David believes that there are no prizes for being miserable at work.

David is an Agile Coach who stumbled across Agile without realising it and has since become a Certified Scrum Professional, Certified Scrum Master, Certified Scrum Product Owner, a Certified Lean Kanban practitioner a Certified LeSS Practitioner, Certified Agile Leader and an ICAgile Certified Professional.

David started his IT career at Reuters where he worked as a Product Manager and successfully launched a number of ground-breaking, new products.

Since moving on from Reuters, David has consulted at a number of high profile organisations including Qualcomm, Vodafone, Barclays, Ovo Energy, Visa and HSBC. In each case David has introduced and developed new ways of working across large programmes of work. His goals have always been to improve the companies' ability to deliver value to their customers as well as to improve the working lives of its staff by giving them a renewed purpose.

David is based in the UK and is married with two children. After enjoying time with his family, he spends the spare time that is left swimming in the sea and running through the New Forest.

www.linkedin.com/in/david-smith-coach

When Being Agile Is Not Enough

Ahmed Syed

My Wednesday 8.30am meeting with the Head of Department had become a sacred ritual. This was no typical meeting. Robin is an intellectual giant and the meeting felt more like a game of professional baseball with concepts, ideas and challenges constantly being pitched and caught. Topics ranged from humanities, psychology, neuroscience and engineering – no topic was off the cards. I was like a kid in a candy store. I felt privileged; honoured even, but as I entered the bathroom that May of 2018, on my way to the meeting, I knew today would be different.

The uncontrollable sobbing coming from the cubicle quickly turned into a feigned cough on hearing my presence. A grown man in his mid-30s hurriedly opened the cubicle looking to escape, his head lowered as his embarrassed eyes met mine. Concern turned to shock as I recognised the piercing eyes of my team mate: Ben. Surely things hadn't got to this?

In the 1800s this organisation was innovating, that was before even I was born.

Shocking. Alex innovated around the thickness of the paper of its law books, creating a paper so thin and light that rather than carry a veritable wheel barrow of books, lawyers where now able to carry all their precedents and case law in a single hard bound book.

Sometimes it feels like innovation is something new. It isn't really, it's in our DNA, it's been around since the dawn of mankind.

However, times have changed since the industrial revolution, and this digital data revolution feels as though it is moving at a breath-taking pace, but I'm sure witnesses of prior revolutions would have attested to the same feeling.

Now, this once unchallenged giant of the legal publishing world, had serious competition. Customer demands were expanding at a dizzying pace whilst new upstarts clambered to find a way to satisfy these demands. All this meant that *Alexo's* market share was rapidly dwindling. What made this worse was that each customer lost was a multi-million pound loss, and the multi-year tie-ins with competitors meant there was no prospect of winning them back for some years, exacerbating the sense of dread felt with each loss. However, there was something far more damaging then just a loss in revenue. *Alexo* and its competitors where building the next generation legal eco-system. Think of it as the *Betamax* and the *VHS* format wars of the 1980s or for you millennials, the *Google Android* vs *Apple IOS* wars. Each customer loss was a vote of confidence for an alternate eco-system: the stakes could not have been higher.

I grabbed Ben by the arm and asked him to come with me to another room. I was worried. I was embarrassed. I was the Agile coach. I have team members I am coaching crying in the bathroom. I have failed them. This was one area I didn't want to fail fast in or indeed fail at all. Real lives where at stake, lives I cared about, lives I was responsible for.

I went to the coffee machine and got him a warm drink. He sipped at the coffee eagerly, perhaps pleased for the distraction more than the coffee. He slipped back into the couch. "It wasn't supposed to be like this. I feel that I am just not good enough for what is needed."

"What's brought this on Ben? You are a key contributor to the team. I know there is a lot of pressure, but you are creating a lot of value and everyone really appreciates what you are doing." No, you're wrong, Ahmed. It's just not so simple, people don't see things the way you do and with that he got up and left." I sat there quietly, puzzled and reflecting on just what had happened. "This isn't going to be so simple," I thought.

This reminded me of my puzzling introduction to the organisation just four months earlier. Here was a company using an Agile delivery methodology, teams working to what most would consider a good Agile standard. Sure, they weren't hyper performing teams, but I had seen worse; far worse.

So here we had 13 agile teams, running *Scrum* or *Kanban* shipping potentially shippable products every sprint, running effective ceremonies, highly skilled - in many cases *dream team* level of skills. Great artefacts, from backlogs to metrics with a real understanding of their capacity, great interaction between the *Product Owners* and the rest of the team. Yet this organisation was entirely ineffective in its ability to release anything of relevance to the market. In the past 18 months, this organisation had released absolutely nothing: something was wrong somewhere, and it was my job to find it ...

A flurry of interactions and interventions with individuals and teams ensued providing recommendations for improvements which by and large where adopted by the teams eager to improve. This was good, but sadly, would prove to be not enough.

Everywhere I went I could see evidence of accumulating debt: the silent insidious type. The kind that had killed many a host silently with ruthless efficiency. Small, seemingly insignificant decisions made some time ago without a thought of the long-term organisational impact where now being felt. Decisions made for ease rather than to further the organisations mission.

Sarah was clearly an impressive director, articulate and poised under pressure. The meeting was called in haste, and she wasted no time in getting to the point.

"Our organisation is building the next generation of legal search and content repository. The idea is simple, but its execution is anything but ... case law, precedents, commentary and other legal information is constantly being compiled and updated by our staff in editorial systems around the world and this information is provided to lawyers in a user friendly and consumable offering, providing real time search together with a rich supporting commentary."

She went on to explain that over the past 15 years, geographically dispersed functions had been given a high degree of autonomy, leading to significant improvements in the provision of legal solution services to local markets. However, it also resulted in a plethora of confused and divergent offerings and systems.

I left the meeting oddly elated, things were finally starting to fall into place, essentially from what I had witnessed and conversations with leaders such as Sarah, there were just five main problems:

1. **Disruption to the flow of value.** Teams were releasing functionality which made the most sense from their local system or function point of view, but how this fitted in to the overall value stream was not clear. No one had an overall handle on what constituted value to the end user, and functionality was decided in a very siloed fashion.

2. **Hero Driven Development.** It turned out that Ben, was in a state due to the constant beratement of one of the top developers in Europe. We had sacrificed team players for heroes. Heroes where seen to be the main creators of value rather than the team. They were propping up the teams on one end and draining them of vitality and creativity on the other.

3. **Incongruent Market Offerings.** Essentially one part of the organisation was undoing the work being done in another. Rather than pulling in one direction, they had almost as many directions as geographic regions.

4. **Duplication of systems.** Over the years each regional office had built their own editorial systems, doing the same thing – well, to be accurate, nearly the same thing, each done in a slightly different way, using a unique approach, requiring a unique support offering. This was waste on a mammoth scale. Sure, many of these teams where using an Agile framework of one sort or another, trying to squeeze out micro-efficiencies within the process and technology each iteration, but the overall strategy was flawed. Many were building systems which probably weren't needed in the first place.

5. **Fiefdoms.** The content pipeline from editorial input to end user consumption on the target platform was a long, meandering and confused hodgepodge of systems, protocols, technologies strung together at some point in the past to deliver what was the most important functionality at the time. The pipeline was truly global with data being pushed around the world without rhyme or reason. Each section of the pipeline had a fiefdom 'protecting' assets and corresponding teams.

Over the coming months a number of changes took place to help with these challenges and importantly make the team environment happy once again. Collectively we found the solution to be less about Agile ceremonies, processes and events and more to be focussed around working together, having a clear and understandable vision spanning silos, clearly and regularly being disseminated and reducing the emphasis on heroes.

We found five areas that helped turn this situation from a crisis into something we could be proud of:

1. **Value Stream Identification.** Identification of the true value stream together with aligned prioritisation to ensure that end user value crossing organisation and functional silos was released in a co-ordinated and integrated fashion.

2. **Clarity of purpose and vision.** Teams for the first time could see how they contributed to the bigger picture, rekindling a belief that it was possible to release value spanning teams, systems and silos.

3. **Stop building stuff that isn't needed.** We stopped building isolated systems to find common purpose and re-usability whilst maintaining local flexibility using services. In short, we stopped building things that weren't needed.

4. **No more heroes.** The focus on bringing in individuals who were highly skilled, yet not team players, meant that in pockets, a hero culture could flourish. Encouraging a change in behaviour and where necessary changing out the individuals helped to send a message that team work and supporting one another was a key part of the 'working arrangement' and promoted a focus on team performance rather than individual performance.

5. **Alignment across teams**. Focussing on offerings to market rather than delivery by silo. This global organisation had each local function operating in a silo divorced from each other. Delivery alignment through integrated backlogs, integrated releases and an integrated vision meant that these teams could now collectively release real value through greater alignment.

We focus so much on efficiency, and adherence to the *Agile* process that we forget to ask whether what we are doing is the right thing in the first place.

A collection of teams working in an *Agile* way is not enough to guarantee success.

Knowing your organisations purpose and creating a unified

vision spanning organisational silo together with cross-team collaboration is essential to delivering value and maintaining market relevance. *Nokia's* high performing *Agile* teams, did not stop it from losing huge market share to *Apple* and *Google* in the upper end of the smart phone market.

Being *Agile* is not enough.

* Dates, names and details have been changed for privacy.

About Ahmed Syed

Ahmed is a consultant, international speaker, trainer and advisor specialising in Scaling Agile and embedding an Agile mind-set and culture within organisations.

An experienced *Enterprise Agile Coach, Scaled Agile Release Train Engineer* and *Safe Certified Trainer* with over 20 years of experience, ten years of which has been gained working in Agile environments on business critical projects and programmes. He has led successful Agile transformations, quality and training programmes, spoken at leading conferences, and has an exemplary project and programme delivery record across multiple industries.

Ahmed is also focused on integrating his two passions: neuroscience and software with the aim of impacting the future direction of Agile software delivery. He is the creator of *Agile Mindset Practices*, and is a researcher in brain and mind sciences, and is passionate about taking the latest breakthroughs from brain research and applying them to Agile software delivery.

He runs both certified and non-certified Agile training courses from his consultancy *Sprint 0 Solutions* and can be contacted at

www.sprint0.com

https://www.linkedin.com/in/ahmedasyed/

Customer Collaboration
Over Contract Negotiation

Getting Folks In The World Of Agility To Lead By Example

John Coleman

Leyla is a senior leader based in New York. She leads agility transformation at this major food company. I'm on the ground for two weeks so far. I'm picking up from where some excellent coaches left things, even if what they did was too prescriptive to be sustainable for my liking. A lot of good work done, a lot more to do as Leyla says.

Leyla is a top performer; she is confident, she has a presence, and she is very engaging. Leyla commands attention and respect in every room I've seen her in so far.

Leyla has overseen a viral contagion of unsustainable *Scrum* team pilots. Leyla is pleased with the appetite for change, and it's starting to feel like maybe we're running ahead of ourselves. Leyla paraphrases; "Some say tell the people we depend on outside the *Scrum* teams we are doing *Scrum* so line up and work to our timelines. That won't end well. I say we need to reach out and negotiate a new way."

Leyla had arrived onsite with an MBB (one of McKinsey, Bain & Co. or BCG) consultant. I smile to myself as I see the MBB consultant immediately getting face time and dinner with the CEO and her -1s. Lara is one of the coolest MBBs I have come across. We chatted about Monte Carlo probabilistic forecasting, and she knew more about it than most.

We connected immediately. Full respect to Lara, she gets to eat at the big tables. I am happy that Leyla is asking me for some help. It's a good sign. I agree to meet Leyla in a local bar.

The atmosphere in the bar was electric.

"What would you like to drink, Leyla?" I ask.

Leyla insists "What are you having?" She orders me a glass of Merlot and has a go at me. "What kind of Irish man are you anyway, we're in a bar with the finest of beers, and you drink wine?" We've got to fix this; this is an impediment!", she jests.

Leyla then gets serious then and says, "So when I asked today how you felt about the pilots, John, you mentioned that you think we're in a bubble that's going to burst, and that we have to get more adult about how we grow this thing, right?"

Leyla is keenly listening for my answer, as she indicates through her body language that she agrees. I don't know how Leyla is managing to hear, as the band is starting to play in the bar. I know I don't have much time as our work colleagues might join us later. My 1:1 time is running low.

"Yes, Leyla. I watched a PR video. It featured the Everest product teams. Only the *Product Owner* and one team member are the same out of 20 or so people, and that PR video is just a few months old".

I start again, "Are we committed to having a product organization? I'm all for fresh blood every now and again, but we seem to be at the other extreme, changing people every week!". I pause. Leyla indicates I should continue. "Have we got *whack-a-mole* style management here?".

Leyla reacts, "Yes, I think we do. How do we get people out of those *whack-a-mole* habits? Do we need to get fully prepared first?".

I respond, "Well, Leyla, I read a wonderful article from Leandro Herrero (Herrero, 2018) last week. He wrote a book called *Viral Change* (Herrero, 2008).

In his recent article, Herrero said something like this *can you remember any revolution where the revolutionaries waited for alignment, waited for everything to be in place before starting the revolution?*. Leyla cracks a big smile.

"Consider a pendulum, on one end of the swing of the pendulum, is the bubble, on the other is total preparedness. We need to aim for somewhere in the middle, and we need to embrace the uncertainty. We're looking for people to proactively volunteer for the change. You must have heard stories of some people being delighted to escape the change".

"Yes, I have," Leyla says". I continue. "Having the CEO attend every sprint review is not sustainable. We need the real customer end users there".

Leyla makes a request. "We're doing an *Request for Proposal (RFP)* at the moment for an agile transformation and scaling. You made very insightful comments in the last few days. What do you think needs to be in the RFP?".

"Well Leyla, I get the language as most people use it, so I'll indulge you. I normally talk about growing agility sustainably. What's the purpose though?".

Leyla is smart and says "I know that reducing costs is an indirect outcome, so I would say we need to improve the delivery of customer value and reduce end to end customer lead-time".

I don't tell Leyla yet how I privately worry that the execs are looking at "taking out headcount" to reduce costs, which according to John Seddon causes *Failure Demand* with a knock-on-effect of an increase in long-term costs (Seddon, 2014). *Failure Demand* is something we didn't do right for the customer that is now causing distraction from value demand. The week before the *Chief Financial Officer* admitted as much to me, which I found refreshing (that it was not sugar coated). She is not alone in thinking like that in the exec team. Unlearning is needed for sure.

"OK, cool" I reply. "You know that it's a multi-year journey right, like maybe even ten years or longer".

Leyla gets it. "Well, I'm saying three years, and yes I do get what you're saying, John".

Here's what I recommended for the RFP for a product-oriented organisation like Leyla's:

- Hire the very best independent *agilist* who is also well read/practised in the world of human factors. Hire only one. Let her partner with the CEO. Give her power, to reduce drag. Influencing takes too long and is still needed. Avoid certified change management professionals, as they studied pre-1997 material for-the-most-part. Avoid specialist *Agile Coach* positions. Hire *Agile Coaches* as *Scrum Masters* even if you decide to use *Kanban*.

- Embed the execs in a 9-12 month unlearning program going Beyond *Command and Control, Beyond Budgeting,* really understanding *Professional Scrum,* optimizing the quantity and quality of organizational work in progress, discovering descaling and scaling options, Lean business cases, repetitive practice to allow leaders to become coaches, removing management responsibility to allow managers become leaders, *Viral Change* to tap into social proof, moving from individual performance management to organizational performance management, moving from huge bets to small bets. Get the top thought leaders in to help with this program. At the very least, arrange phone calls with those top thought leaders. Add positive peer review to the program, setting expectations that reading and progress is expected. *Leaders Eat Last, Triggers* and *How Women Rise* will be on the agenda.

- Do the same with middle management/leadership.

- Ensure that exec leaders are prepared to re-organize so that only people who want to be part of the change are part of the change.

- Per product get a *Scrum Master* with exec credibility and successful track record to pair with a senior leader to plot and scheme together as peers. The senior leader will understand the people, the context, and the politics. The coach will realise agility growth, as a rather special *Scrum Master.*

- Find the right synchronisation patterns for teams for each product. Get help from a *Large Scale Scrum* (also known as *LeSS*) coach to define the product(s), even if you don't plan to use *LeSS.*

- Flipping the system tends to lead to higher chances of the change sticking. You can get this from *Large Scale Scrum* (The *LeSS Company,* 2007-2018) or *Tipping Point Leadership* (Gladwell, 2002). LeSS has been around for at least ten years, and it helps with a redesign of the organisation. *Tipping Point Leadership* drives the change through the organisation without convincing people of the goodness of the change, through positive peer pressure. Bratton in NYPD encouraged precinct commissioners to have positive peer review every two weeks on crime figures and he had direct video calls into beat cops' daily briefings. *Tipping Point Leadership* needs proactive support from the very top.

- Understand that the combination of *Waterfall* and *Scrum* is the best of both worlds *(WaterScrumFall)* is a thinking mistake; it leads to the use of best practice for complex work. Complex work needs emergent practice. We can (avoid *WaterScrumFall)* is a choice. Sincere efforts are needed to break away from *WaterScrumFall.* If the choice is we cannot then I would prefer not to be part this, as it drives the opposite of what is needed. That said, I find that clients tend not to be honest even with themselves on that one. A *Program Director* asking for real agility is akin to a turkey voting for Christmas.

Consider a mix of coaches who have the following skills amongst them:

- product definition, self-managing cross-component cross-functional team adoption, informed consent, so people know what they're volunteering for;
- evolutionary self-designing teams;
- setting up and running an executive rhythm for the change;
- improving the flow of customer value;
- hands-on technical excellence, because even if you hate investing in that, you have to for the change to stick;
- openness to multiple approaches, permutations and combinations;
- Go deep and narrow, implementing deep change in a limited area, one area at a time, in a sustainable way. As a last resort, only go for broad & shallow if you need to contain a metaphorical fire, but then quickly begin the deep and narrow journey;
- We need to lead by example, embracing uncertainty. We need to prepare amplification & dampening strategies for every probe/experiment for this change. We'll probably have an emergent zigzag route towards our change vision.

I hope I didn't overload Leyla with that list. It's all very well for me to ask for all that. A real agility chef knows what to do when Leyla metaphorically opens her fridge and she doesn't see much in there for us to cook a truly Agile dish from. I know I need to adapt to the context, particularly the politics. I previously naively believed I could ignore the politics. As a former colleague told me, 'Politics is the art of getting work done".

Leyla says, "I want to benchmark so we can see progress. What should we measure?".

I say "Please avoid story points as they tend to get gamed.

As we progress in time, we can reassess what the organization has the appetite for".

Leyla reacts "OK, but here team happiness is politically valued".

I see this as noise. "Leyla, I'll indulge you for now. Sometimes cranky teams are better as they talk up about impediments. Politically, let's measure it for now".

I get the hint to continue. So, I followed with something like this list:

- # implicit or explicit Product Backlogs, lower is better

Material impact on:

- Delivery of more customer value from the customer perspective
- Reduction of the end to end customer cycle time
- Reduction of failure demand
- Reduction of knowledge/delivery risk
- Happier teams, as it's a political desire in this case (I'm not into this happy-clappy stuff)
- some leading indicators also
- Monitor trends because people tend to game targets and stop continuous improvement after 'meeting' them.
- Implement a consistently reviewed mid/long term spend-rate per product and the complete elimination of projects for fund-raising of product development.
- True establishment of long-term stable teams and one *Product Owner* per product (that a customer can relate to). Short term assignment to Agile teams should be the exception rather than the norm.
- # deprecated traditional roles
- Progress towards a set up of a 40-year career path (Larman,

2017) and rewards program for product developers, *Scrum Masters, Product Owners*, and managers based on the number of materially different skills and the number of skills in which one can coach others. Otherwise, silo career paths will draw people back to their previous silos.

- # *compliance folks* meeting product teams monthly

Leyla interjects, "What about the distraction of political noise, how do we keep the end in mind".

It feels like it's time to reiterate unlearning. We see and hear what we believe. So, I recommend:

- A program of senior/mid-level leadership education on autonomy/alignment, servant leadership, systems thinking, improving flow, making *smaller bets*, continuous improvement, and a small set of professional coaching skills.
- Removing responsibility from management, so they have room to be coaching leaders instead.

I continue, "I'll get a good sense of how serious the senior/mid-level leaders are about the change. There is a whole gambit of skills to learn and unlearn. It's like a multi-year journey. Some leaders only look for tooling for the new world. If so, that might be an indication that we have some *NoNo* characters (John Kotter and Holger Rathgeber, 2016) or *whack-a-mole* (Woodlock, 2012) characters, people who might not be worth investing change energy in much more. This point leads me to think about how people are motivated to collaborate and co-operate. Did we have any silos measures driving a lack of oneness? Do we measure the speed of the baton or the speed of the runners here?".

Leyla seems comfortable with this question, "We have cascaded objectives, it helps to ensure alignment."

I sigh, "I'm sorry Leyla, they have to go, as they drive annual individual performance reviews. Deming used to say, 'Did you know 50% of people perform below average?'" (Deming, 1986).

Leyla gets the joke. "We'll need to look at some of the cooler alignment approaches like intent-based-leadership from David Marquet (Marquet, 2013), or something like that. Also, what about vendors? They'll also need to change, and that's not so easy. How do we motivate vendors through our contracts?"

"Don't talk to me about vendors", Leyla groans. I think that sounds like an Irish figure of speech meaning the opposite of what it sounds like.

'Does Leyla have Irish blood?' I wonder to myself.

Leyla continues, "We avoid fixed priced contracts, and yet we see vendor management folks slicing up their people like they're pizzas as though there are no task-switching costs".

I respond, "It's time to bring everything back in, including agile coaching. I'll bet you dinner, at the most expensive restaurant in town. I am willing to bet that this outsourcing business has higher costs in the long term. Also, I'll wager that the baton is slower than it was. Am I right?".

"No need for a bet", Leyla sighs.

"OK", I respond, "There is a lot of work to do here, let's build up internal capability, step by step. Who knows? Maybe the vendors will work with us like we're just one family, but only if we have long-term arrangements, none of this retendering every 6-12 months I see in other places please".

"What about compensation?", Leyla says.

I think I'm running out of time with this 1:1. Emily across the bar signals to us that she will come over to us.

"It's important to let people keep their current compensation packages, including company car, even if they move from line management into being a *Product Developer*. Reduction of cost is not our optimizing goal; it should arise as an indirect outcome later from the better flow of customer value. Let's see how things play out. 'It's complex, therefore let's probe.' as Dave Snowden would say. You remember? We talked about the *Cynefin* sense-making framework right?" (Snowden, 2010).

"Great videos, they were funny." Leyla recalls.

"One last thing, we need to embrace uncertainty. We can't plan all of this. We don't know how people will react. We can't even assume what education is needed until we understand the work more. So, let's avoid fixed price contracts for the RFP, we need to lead by example. That also means not chopping and changing *Scrum Masters*. I think the best way to understand all of this is through system modelling".

I started drawing an example of a simple system model on a beer mat…

"Hey Emily, how are you doing?". Emily is *Product Owner*, probably our best.

"Oh, I recognize that. John facilitated the drawing of a system model for us; it helped our thinking. But let's have fun now eh!". Emily is right, and it's time for me to order this time.

"What would you like to drink Emily? And Leyla, how about you?", I ask.

Emily and Leyla tell me their drink orders. Before I turn to the bar, I say with a big smile "Let's leave the system model until Monday anyhow, we need more than the space of a beermat".

"Speaking of drinks," Leyla says, "no more of that wine business … ".

I consider how mindful and enjoyable that conversation was before I order at the bar. It's great to feel a sense of co-operation, pull, and respect. I see a real opportunity. For the first time in years, the appetite for change is massive, caused by an existential crisis.

Bibliography

- Deming, W. E., 1986. *Out of the Crisis.* s.l.:s.n.

- Gladwell, M., 2002. *The Tipping Point: How Little Things Can Make a Big Difference.* s.l.:s.n.

- Herrero, D. L., 2008. *Viral Change.* 2nd edition ed. s.l.:s.n.

- Seddon, J., 2014. *The Whitehall Effect: How Whitehall Became the Enemy of Great Public Services - and What We Can Do About it.* s.l.:Triarchy Press.

- Herrero, L., 2018. *The organization (re)volution will be postponed. Once more.* [Online]
Available at: https://leandroherrero.com/the-organization-revolution-will-be-postponed/[Accessed 9 March 2018].

- John Kotter and Holger Rathgeber, 2016. *Our Iceberg Is Melting: Changing and Succeeding Under Any Conditions.* 10th-anniversary ed. s.l.:s.n.

- Larman, C., 2017. *Craig Larman's unique brand of Certified LeSS Practitioner training where Craig covers adoption topics not seen in any book anywhere.* Philadelphia, Pennsylvania, USA, Craig Larman.

- Magennis, T., 2011. *Forecasting and Simulating Software Development Projects: Effective Modeling of Kanban & Scrum Projects using Monte-Carlo Simulation.* s.l.:s.n.

- Marquet, L. D., 2013. *Turn the Ship Around! A True Story of Building Leaders by Breaking the Rules.* s.l.:s.n.

- Snowden, D., 2010. *Cynefin Sense-Making Framework.* [Online]
Available at: https://www.youtube.com/watch?v=N7oz366X0-8 [Accessed 9 March 2018].

- The LeSS Company, 2007-2018. *Large Scale Scrum (LeSS).* [Online] Available at: http://www.less.works [Accessed 9 March 2018].

- Woodlock, D., 2012. *Intro to System Dynamics Video* 13d -

Whack-a-Mole. [Online] Available at: https://www.youtube.com/watch?v=Ed1V7LZrsWM [Accessed 9 March 2018].

Dedication

To Vanesa Cernamorit, Magdalena Cersamba, Adam Coleman, Antoinette Coleman, Emily Coleman, Lara Coleman, William Coleman – none of whom understand what I do. They are not alone.

In the year of #*Me too* and the week of writing, the week of *International Women's Day,* all the characters other than John Coleman are women. John Coleman looks forward to the day when attention does not need to be drawn to this point.

John Coleman also wishes to thank three of the people in the agility world for whom John holds in the highest regards: the reviewers Nader Talai, Simon Ashdown, and James Scrimshire. Their grasp of the topics and their attention to detail was a fantastic addition to this piece.

About John Coleman

John Coleman is a *Professional Scrum Trainer* (including *Kanban*), a *LeSS Friendly Scrum* trainer, a candidate *LeSS* trainer, and a member of *Marshall Goldsmith's Lead60 Group.*

John Coleman likes to help organizations to *ACe* their agility towards their optimizing goals. John helps the new kids on the block to become experts in agility and transformation. John helps to develop new agility chefs, budding experts in both agility and transformation, two separate bodies of knowledge.

John works at all levels, with teams, with products/service teams and exec level. John is a systems thinker, and most importantly, John takes an independent view. John specializes in the human factors.

John's *Scrum+Kanban* case studies can be found on *www.scrumcasestudies.com* (international payments company, European bank).

John helps leaders and teams. His executive leadership for agility unlearning program gets rave reviews.

https://www.linkedin.com/in/johncolemanagilitychef/

john@ace.works

@johncolemanirl

Responding To Change
Over Following A Plan

Oh Come All Ye Faithful

Mike Nuttall

"Without Agile we are nothing

Without Scrum we are lost

Without retrospective we don't improve

Go team!"

Luthor The High Priest, (2017),
What will I do today http://www.churchofagile.org

For a long, long time I was a devout believer in methodologies. For me, they brought order where there had been chaos, predictability instead of uncertainty, and rules where anarchy threatened. They also seemed to work as a way of getting stuff done. So, for a time, when *Agile* became the new way of doing things, *Scrum* was my methodology of choice. I practiced *Scrum*, got certified in *Scrum*, got employed on the basis of my experience with *Scrum* and I did my utmost to make sure the rituals that embodied *Scrum* were followed wherever I went (within reason). However, my experience a few years ago, ironically in a role that I secured in no small part due to my *Scrum* knowledge, totally changed my view.

On a sunny July afternoon not many years ago I sat in a meeting room at a fast growing Shoreditch start up. Well, start up is a bit of a stretch. The company was already seven years old, was trading in the tens of millions and had around 100 employees. They were growing fast and very focused on maintaining an open, collaborative culture. But all was not rosy. I listened to their CEO recount the many problems they faced with their *so called Agile* development teams.

'It's like they're believers of the *church of Agile*, but none of the rest of us know what it's all about', he told me, ' and all I know is that nothing ever seems to come out the other side.'

Fast forward a couple of months, I've taken the job and am starting to learn what he meant.

I'd expected to find a business that was yet to understand agile delivery approaches, was doing some form of *Fragile*, or faced resistance caused by senior staff wanting to micro-manage delivery, but none of these things were really at the centre of the problems. Unusually, at least for me, the situation was not one of lack of support for agile methods, or a lack of understanding. Engineering was running how they wanted to run. They had heavily invested in complex workflows, meticulously and expensively implemented and maintained in *Jira*, and had an unswerving commitment to the rituals and machinery of *Scrum*. Nobody was telling them not to operate that way. This should have been *Scrum* nirvana, no?

But pretty much nobody was happy with the results.

How did this all look? Teams were abstract, each with its own animal name and they would rotate off one project when finished onto whatever was next in the priority queue. Unfortunately this didn't happen often. Who exactly was responsible for setting priorities was not terribly well understood. Another side effect of abstract teams was that all engineers had to be explicitly full stack, generalists with no specialisms allowed.

So, on one hand we had lots of frustrated business leaders sharing the view that nothing of value ever got delivered. On the other, an engineering team who felt they had tried hard to be the very model of modern agile software development, but were undervalued and much maligned.

Previous attempts to fix it had involved hiring lots of extra people into hierarchical disciplines. Lots of *UI, UX,* design heads were employed to try and smooth the path to delivering projects, and when that didn't work, a PMO was created, sitting under the COO, and tasked with herding the cats. The rationale being that imposing some structure and discipline from above would help marshal all that *Agile.* Maybe put *Scrum* under a *Waterfall?*

My task (not undertaken alone, by any stretch) was to nudge, course correct and persuade the project delivery organisation, as it was seen at the time, into being something that the business valued and appreciated.

Add to the mix that the company's engineering platform was old, unreliable and monolithic and there was the added challenge to find mechanisms that would allow people to deliver value to the business without having to stop dead while re-engineering the whole thing from the ground up.

The first thing that needed attention looked like *Scrum* itself. Agile was being viewed as a methodology, and *Scrum* as it's testaments. Working with the *Chief Product Officer,* we started to formulate a view that stripping away the processes, workflows and diktats might offer a better future. We wanted to give people something to care about so they could collectively decide how to bring benefit, not force people to abide by a set of rules they had never signed up to. Less explicitly, we wanted stop people thinking in terms of projects altogether.

The aim was to break down some of the hierarchical barriers that had grown and put together teams that could properly take charge of a *thing,* a subdomain or problem area of appropriate size. *Engineering* and *Product* were prepared to kick over some statues and we hoped that other disciplines could be gently persuaded to come along.

It was not quite this:

'Get rid of everything. Get rid of your scrum master, your product owner, your *Agile* coach, and fire the *Agile* consultancy that's going to make you more *Agile*. Now that you have a blank slate you can start to figure out what makes sense for YOU.'

Amir Yasin, (2015), *Agile Is The New Waterfall,* Medium.com

But there was a sense that '*Big A*' *Agile* was not helping.

Team names were abandoned, *Jira* workflows retired and we let teams decide how they wanted to work and what they wanted to call themselves, if anything. Some *Kanban* emerged (temporarily, it turned out) to support a sense of momentum, and physical boards became prevalent. Without explicitly mandating it, we encouraged teams to look for some quick wins to earn trust capital with their stakeholders.

To support change, leaders were encouraged to step back from imposing process and instead encourage teams to try what felt right.

We continually tried to keep a focus on a culture of collaboration over allegiance to functional disciplines, CPO and VP of *Engineering* hoping to lead by example to the rest of senior team. We wanted to show that we didn't believe it was necessary to *own* the people but instead to take responsibility for looking after that set of skills on behalf of the business, helping employees develop, giving them career direction, and providing forums to talk about things that mattered to them in their roles.

Attitudes and process around hiring were also altered, encouraging more diversity, across all dimensions, and a preference for potential and energy over perfect skill set or experience.

Change did start to come, tangible results emerged and it felt there was a growing enthusiasm for the new shape of teams. However, there were plenty of problems along the way. Not replacing the platform meant we always carried an overhead both in terms of new features, but also in dealing with failures. We let the teams decide whether their challenges required shiny new stuff built or whether they could make do and mend. We also strongly urged them to be good neighbours and not make technical decisions that could hurt anyone else, encouraging explicit ownership of services and features, and abiding to a moral contract for their use.

Some people hated the change and left, and there were almost certainly more fights, tears, tantrums and toys thrown than if we'd let a PMO do things, but a lot of people probably grew an inch or two when they realised they were genuinely being allowed to make decisions.

The tendency from leadership to ask for more structure never altogether disappeared, and any new member of the senior team invariably started out as a disbeliever. Gentle persuasion that it would more than likely be OK was the most effective way of dealing with these challenges.

You would probably, rightly, suggest though we hadn't really done anything, and we certainly never had a firm plan. Structure and process had been removed and people encouraged to take responsibility, but importantly they were also given the belief that people in the senior team had their backs. An internal metaphor emerged; it was OK to pull cat's tails, but not stick forks in electrical sockets. Without ever stating it as a goal, *Agile* stopped being important, and *agility* became the norm.

That sense of ownership and responsibility that grew in the teams did produce very positive results. Over three years the business tripled in size, with a large part of that growth attributable to the teams moving dials on key metrics and delivering new product or features. In parallel, the culture of the company evolved into one where cross disciplinary collaboration became central to how things get done. From an engineering viewpoint, a culturally diverse team of specialist generalists emerged who understood the business they worked in and how they, as individuals, could contribute to its success.

So, what lessons were learnt? Care less about the scripture and more about the underlying values. Make sure leadership seek to lead, not command. Complicated processes are not always the answer to complex problems. Smart people can be trusted to do the right thing. Soft lessons all of them, but human situations are often more *EQ* than *IQ* in the end.

About Mike Nuttall

Mike Nuttall is currently *Head of Technology* at *Pottermore.com* and *CTO in Residence* at UCL School Of Management. He has held *CTO, VP Engineering* and *VP Technology* positions in a number of successful and not so successful start ups. He started out as a very bad programmer, progressed to being a somewhat more capable project  manager and later found he enjoyed and appeared to be not too terrible at engineering management.

He's worked across many methodologies and frameworks over the years from Information Engineering to SSADM to DSDM and more.

For the last ten years or more he's largely been running engineering intermingled in interdisciplinary product engineering teams and trying to find ways of being agile and delivering value, sometimes with success.

https://www.linkedin.com/in/mikeynuttall/

Breaking Free Of The Plan

Bruce Thompson

I was watching a sushi chef. They worked calmly and precisely. Cutting just enough fish, working quickly, but not rushing. Finishing each piece completely, cleaning down their station and moving on to the next order. Actually, it was a whole brigade of chefs, all working together, synchronised with economical words, to deliver the beautiful food.

They were an amazing team.

Perhaps one day when I cook it will be like that, but as much as I aspire to such orderly calm, I always end up with a bit of a rush at the end, distracted by unexpected events and adapting things at the last minute. I always plan to do too much and over commit. There is no way I can work in a team when I'm cooking. I have to concentrate so hard on timings and recipes that there is no mental space left over to co-ordinate with other people. I am a barely verbal cook, culinary mutism. I enjoy it though, once it is done and the stress is over.

I have always enjoyed software development too. First as a developer, then a team leader and more recently as a senior manager. And like with cooking, I have learned mostly from experience, but unlike cooking I have aspired to professionalism and worked hard to emulate the precision and efficiency I observed in the sushi chef and their team. It was not easy, particularly given that my natural inclinations are to overcommit and compensate with brute force hard work, resulting in plenty of stress that reduces my communication and makes teamwork a challenge.

Watching the chefs got me thinking about one of my earlier projects, one where I think I really started to properly internalise the difference between being truly agile and just dabbling.

Before this project if you had asked me: are you agile? I would have answered with resounding agreement. I certainly believed in the agile values, even if I had a limited understanding of them. And I had had success running projects using various iterative, goal-oriented project management approaches. These successes had led to being given responsibility for larger and larger projects. This was great, but the projects were also getting harder to manage and I was finding it increasingly difficult to keep up.

My tipping point was about a quarter through an ambitious, highly technical project with a large team. The project had gone very well initially, so well that the scope had increased as it started to appear likely that we would be able to deliver more than expected. Small changes in scope can bring much larger changes in complexity and this was the case here. I found myself feeling like a victim of my own success. Everyone seemed to believe we would deliver, but I was increasingly unsure that we would. Those small changes in scope had increased the technical complexity to a level that was very hard to manage using the toolkit that had always worked for me in the past.

My career began in architecture – the one with bricks – and this has brought me some great benefits, but also some bad habits. Architecture students at my university saw it as a badge of honour to work long hours. Architects are expected to own the whole overall design of a building, and it is taken as read that even though the details might be worked out as you construct the building, the high-level design is not. You set yourself a stretch goal, sell the vision and then deliver through blood, sweat and tears.

Armed with these bad habits, I had taken on far too much technical design responsibility. When project sponsors wanted commitment to high level designs up front, I gave it. Then, as the design increased in complexity and took more effort to maintain, I had tried to *power through* with longer hours. This lead, inevitably, to higher stress levels that lead to me communicating less often and less clearly, undermining my team's ability to support me. Because I now had a lot of the design in my head, I was the only one who could manage the plans and divvy up the work.

I knew all about the anti-pattern of the coding hero – but I'd fallen into the trap anyway. My ego got the better of me; and my ego was also getting in the way of getting me out of it. I was full of doubt, but I didn't want to admit it to anyone.

I got pretty desperate. I was reduced to doing something radically out of character for me at the time, something which I have subsequently come to see as a bit of super power. I asked for help. (I still won't ask for directions though – I have limits).

Help arrived over several days of meetings in the canteen with a wonderfully talented member of my team whose skills I really didn't appreciate fully at the time. They sat me down with pen, paper and coffee and said: "How will the whole project look when it is done? Draw the whole thing." It really was all in my head, so I was able to draw it out. It took a few goes to get the detail right, but quite quickly we had the overview. This was a drawing I had been *definitely going to do tomorrow* for several weeks. It was the key to enabling the rest of the team to carry more load, but I hadn't understood how important this was. I was always too busy spinning other plates to complete this task.

Now they asked: "How would you split this into two parts, a first release and a second release?" It was simple enough to make this split. I shaded in the elements that needed to be delivered first. Then they removed the later release from the design picture entirely: "Ok, imagine this is all we will deliver. How much value would it have? How would you split this into a release with most of that value and a follow up release to *finish off?*" with a bit of thought I could split the design further. And this was repeated a couple more times until we had identified several releasable phases, each delivering the next most valuable features. And the first one was a fraction of the whole, but actually had a lot of the value. This will come as no surprise to seasoned agile developers; but it was a huge surprise to me at the time; actually, I didn't really believe it would work, but I could see I had nothing to lose by doing release one first.

I didn't know I was being coached at the time; but in hindsight this was my first experience of working with a skilled coach. I knew where the value was and I knew how to express the design on paper, but I need help to actually do it.

Over the course of two days, I had gone from being on the path to failure, lost in a forest of endless detail, to being having a clear direction and an achievable, visible goal. The simplified first release scope was much more tractable to deliver. By breaking the project apart into an overall vision, but defining the narrowest possible first release we gained three benefits:

1. **Focus.** When the first deliverable is also the only deliverable, you have to worry about every detail, of every element, all the time. Everyone and every team has an upper limit to how much complexity they can manage. In my case I had exceeded this limit and the effect was overwhelming me, leading to a communication breakdown that disabled the team and put the project at risk. It is much better to deliver a tangible benefit with real value that the team can understand and communicate about, than to fail to deliver a grand vision.

2. **Vision.** Even though we had carved out a smaller area of focus, we still had the grand high-level vision as context. This gave us something to aim for, a reason to want to deliver phase one early. And it reassured the stakeholders that we weren't just

going for quick, tactical wins at the expense of the bigger picture.

3. The vision and the current focus were shared by the whole team. Those drawings went on to become the basis for presentations to the team, the wider technical community and the stakeholders. They became the centrepiece of a shared story. A place to anchor all other discussions. I didn't really appreciate at the time just how important that was; but as I look back I see how this enabled the team to self-organise around delivering the vision.

Equipped with this vision and the first release scope, we set about delivering the project. In the end, there were several more surprises and unexpected delays to work through just to get the first release into the users' hands. It took a lot longer to deliver the first release than I would have ever anticipated; but we still delivered that release earlier than we had projected for delivering the grand vision. Of course, the grand vision would probably have been even more delayed, but that is academic.

Release one was a good one. It had all the highest value features and when business conditions changed unexpectedly, in a way which put those features through a tough real-world test, it passed with flying colours. The later releases were not really needed and effort could be redirected to other high value work.

Looking back, this is the project where I let go of my architect's instinct that there must be a comprehensive grand vision that is delivered as one complete package. I took a leap of faith that you can iterate, delivering the highest value first and learned that sometimes release one is good enough.

It is where I started to see how failing to communicate with the team will derail your project more certainly than whatever it is you think you need to be doing instead of communicating (this one took a while to sink in, maybe still is).

And that getting help, even just a few hours and especially from someone who knows a few coaching tricks, can be the difference between success and failure.

Perhaps I should get some advice on how to be a better cook.

About Bruce Thompson

Bruce Thompson knew he wanted to work with computers from the moment he first saw a *Sinclair ZX81* as an impressionable nine-year old. Combined with love of making things this led Bruce on a path that included architecture (the one with bricks), 4D CAD systems and settled in the financial sector. That passion for technology has evolved into  a passion for helping technology teams deliver innovative solutions to complex business challenges by applying lean and agile thinking.

www.linkedin.com/in/bruce-j-thompson

Change - The Good, The Bad And The Ugly

Jessica Gilbert

Have you ever tried to write code, or predict how long it will take to build something, when you secretly have no idea of the best way to do it? This is a day in the life of a *Software Engineer.*

Most of the time, it's no secret that the team are making it up as they go along. This is not a flaw of the people, just human nature when doing something you've never done before. If you don't know, you can only guess.

We give the team a complicated business problem to solve, and while their brains are still whirring, someone comes along and asks for a plan of how they're going to do it, and roughly what size it is. Admittedly, that someone is usually me!

I've been working in a predominantly business-to-business environment for the last few years, which can significantly change the level of upfront planning required. Unfortunately, in most organisations there is a very real business need to have the size and scope of a piece of work mapped out quite early on, and in a lot of instances the only thing we know with any certainty is that this plan we just made up ... is all going to change!

Should We Embrace Change?

The *agile* principles say, "Welcome changing requirements, even late in development. *Agile* processes harness change for the customer's competitive advantage."

While I'm onboard with the principle, it's not an easy one to get right. Let's talk about some of the common mistakes around adapting to change, and review what I would consider to be the good, the bad and the ugly examples I have run into. At the same time, let's look at how we can adapt to change in an effective way that keeps costs down and productivity high.

The Good

Inspect and Adapt

A good example of adapting to change is allowing a project to evolve and improve throughout its creation cycle. This is discovering a better solution than you first planned. Now you have more information and more time to think about it, you have a fantastic idea to dramatically improve the product.

It's also showing someone what you've just done and receiving feedback that you know will have a positive impact on the end result, at a time where it's still easy enough to accommodate. These types of changes have a net positive impact on both the team and the product. Of course there is a cost associated to these changes, but when it comes to (what we're going to call) productivity tax, you are cashing in. These types of change have a positive impact on the ownership and productivity of the team, mainly because they're driving the change and you've allowed them the freedom and autonomy to do so.

This isn't good because *Agile* says so ... it's just human psychology. People prefer making changes when it's their idea or it's seen as a collaboration to make things better.

For The Customer's Competitive Advantage

There is a key qualifier at the end of our *Agile* principle that forms a large part of this example. "For the customer's competitive advantage"

Example: An industry change factor, or a competitor's actions cause an adaption to project/feature scope.

What's the cost?

If these changes apply to features that haven't been started yet, then the cost of change should be quite minimal. At this point the team shouldn't have invested too much time and effort in them.

If the features are already built, then obviously the cost is higher. But this cost isn't just the time taken to build it. You now need to pay your productivity tax. On this particular request, I would guess it would be a small productivity tax. If those features are already built, you may have to double it.

Why the tax?

Because you have a team of disheartened individuals whose work is going to waste. For the next couple of weeks they're going to be a little bit grumpy about it. The quicker you can get this information passed across, the cheaper the tax. There are two main tax multipliers here.

The first is that everyone needs to believe it couldn't have been avoided or flagged sooner. The second, is that the team need to be as invested in the success of the product as the rest of the organisation. When we get that right, the team will be bought into making the change for the greater good of the business and the product. Let's not forget two things here, most engineers are all about logical reasoning, and nobody wants to work hard on a project that wasn't worth the effort.

We need to be able to react to industry change and the quicker we can do that, the better we are. This is true agility at its best.

The Bad

Customer Feedback

Hang on ... isn't this exactly what the agile principle invited us to do?!? I can see you're already a little bit annoyed this is listed as bad. How is this any different from the good example before?

Because the pre-qualifier for my example is this ... You didn't show the customer until it was finished! I have lost count how many times I've seen this happen and derail teams and roadmaps.

When you hear *Agile* folk talking about how we need to *Implement Agile* across the whole business and not just *Engineering* ... this is a good example of what we mean.

Of course this is still a valid business driven request based on genuine needs. It's just that your net cost and productivity tax is on a sliding scale from 0 - 100%. The question is, *did it really need to be?*

I know you're sick of hearing it, so let's ignore this word *Agile* for a moment. I encourage you to say, "Stop using this word *Agile* and just tell me specifically what you need me to do". I promise you, the requests will make a lot of sense.

To implement it across the wider business, you don't need to use the word *Agile* or send people on a course to understand it, or get certifications and badges that say, "I can do it". You just need to understand that you are now part of the development process too. Enjoy it, embrace it and make time for it. It's very rewarding.

We have a responsibility to explain things to you in a language everybody can understand; hold us to account and make sure we do. That's all part of best practice too.

For us to turn this example from bad to good, the engineering teams are going to show you little and often and ask you for your valuable feedback. Now here's the important bit … Go and show the customer! Or, if you wanted, you could ask to bring the customer to the demo. By doing this now, we can accommodate feedback with minimal tax and minimal cost. It's really important that you show up.

Like you, the clients don't need to understand *Agile* to be part of the process. Just that we need to show them what we've done so far so we can get their feedback on an early prototype. If your client has any power to provide feedback and actually impact change, then you must include them in the evolution.

Often, there is a fear that by showing the customer you are inviting more request for change. You need to decide as a business how much of a stake the customer has in the end result and manage expectations accordingly, but if they have the power to decide the fate and future of the product then the earlier, the better.

The faster the feedback, the cheaper the change in both cost and productivity tax.

We all know keeping clients happy can be exhausting! That's true of every business in any industry. When it's the client's prerogative to change their mind, they will! The goal is to allow them to do that, while keeping frustrations to a minimum.

My final note on this one: More scope, means more time (and possibly more resource). There is no world where feedback doesn't take time to implement. If this is a project with an agreed delivery date, when the client gives you feedback, you need to manage expectations and move the goalposts. Change doesn't come for free. Adapting to change is a two-way thing.

The Ugly

The first time I heard the term *Agile* was back in my first software engineer role. I remember my project manager telling me that Agile was going to allow us to adapt to change ...

Well, three months later and I swore that it was just a golden ticket to allow the business to keep changing its mind! I hated it and I didn't understand it. People seemed to be making it up to suit their own needs. We evolved from there to become a highly performing mature *Agile* team, but that's not the last time in my career I saw adapting to change be a mask for constantly changing our minds in a team that was new to *Agile*.

Later, in another organisation, one of my teams told me that they had chosen to work *Kanban*, so that they could adapt to change. It was admirable, but what I very quickly realised was that the main issue was that the business couldn't fix down its top priorities for a whole two week period.

The team were victims of their own adaptability and in reality just kept taking new top priorities daily. It was a horrible working environment and the team were demotivated, unproductive and certainly didn't feel like they were in control of anything.

In this scenario I had to drill into the business needs and understand why things were constantly changing priority. There were two streams of work coming into this team: one was development work, but the second was maintenance tasks. The maintenance tasks made sense to be worked on in a *Kanban* fashion; they had quite short turnaround times and were single repeatable units of work, but we needed to stabilize the development work.

We later moved to fortnightly sprints to try and regain some stability around the engineering work. We then implemented a separate process for these repeatable tasks that had a genuine business need to be turned around quickly.

Once we had a single funnel for requests, a formalised request process, a business owner prioritising the requests and a maximum number of requests per day, we were good to go. We'd then alternate the responsibility to manage the request queue and keep the workstream separate from the engineering work.

Instantly the team felt in control again. We'd moved the constantly changing priorities out of sight of the team and the health, happiness and productivity of the team went up.

Clearly there was a genuine business need for some of the last-minute requests, but when these were coupled in with engineering work, it was just one big free for all!

Final Thoughts

In all of the examples I've given there's been an underlying business need for the change. My examples were not classified on the validity of the request, but the cost and inefficiencies of the process leading to the change.

Being able to adapt to change doesn't always mean you should. This is not a decision you should make lightly and being Agile doesn't automatically mean you should do so.

The primary objective I have been set in every role I've held in the last five years is to improve productivity. I like to think I'm good at doing exactly that, but change is one of the main contributing factors that impacts productivity and my ability to maintain happy, healthy and motivated teams. In today's current market, hiring and retaining good engineers is the hardest it's ever been. There are more jobs than people and smart people will only work for good companies.

If you want to be on the good side of change, then let's do good, manage bad and avoid ugly.

About Jessica Gilbert

Jessica Gilbert has always loved problem solving. She knew she wanted to be a programmer the first time she spent a whole day tearing her hair out trying to write code. It was the best puzzle she'd ever seen! You tried to build something, and when it didn't work, you just had to follow a logical, methodical route through the code to problem solve it, until it worked! Sometimes this took minutes, sometimes it took hours, but it was always so satisfying when it finally worked.

It's that same love of problem solving that saw her move into *Scrum Mastering* and then *Engineering Management*, except the puzzle has now become people and processes, which it turns out are far more complicated to fix than *Software*, but equally as rewarding!

Jessica is currently *Head of Engineering* at *Masabi,* a ticketing start-up based in London, disrupting the *Transit* industry.

www.linkedin.com/in/gilbertjessica

Customer Focus As A Transformation Vehicle - With Super Powers

John Boyes

Customer focus is a great recipe for a successful *agile transformation*. I'll show this by looking closely at a transformation that I was part of at one of the UK's largest media companies in 2015. I'll also demonstrate how a successful ransformation can only be achieved if you embrace responding to change over following a plan. Get ready for some revelations along the way which may surprise you!

The first thing to highlight about this transformation is that it was conceived primarily as a business transformation. Crucially, it had clear customer-orientated goals from the outset. The main high-level goal, set by the newly-created *Digital Director*, was: to transform the company's bloated website from thousands of static pages into tens of beautiful, simple intelligent pages. A clear goal, set by senior management at the outset, easily understood by everyone involved and with a strong customer focus. *Tick, tick, tick, tick.*

So far, so good, right? Well, not entirely. Although everything above is spot on, there was also a large spanner in the works: the business (i.e. non-technical leadership) didn't bring technology along for the journey from the start.

Instead the design of the all-new website was outsourced to

a small design agency who were to work in splendid isolation from the company's technology teams, and then to hand the *finished* design over to the technology teams nine months later.

Things started off OK: the design agency were one of the better ones around, and after a couple of months had produced a very slick design prototype which was certainly beautiful and simple. But if the designers continued to work in isolation for another seven months before throwing their design over the fence to technology, you could bet your house that the transformation would not end well. Why so? *Big Design Up Front* is not a recipe for success, that's why.

Fortunately, the company's technical leadership had (eventually) been made aware of both the transformation's existence and its current strategy. Even more importantly, they then succeeded in persuading the *Digital Director* that although the *Big Design Up Front* strategy may glimmer for a while, it would ultimately fail. Time to pivot.

The design agency became co-located with one of the company's development teams who were now to work full-time on the transformation with them, along with a dedicated *Product Owner*. I was the *Agile Coach* for the development team, so I was now right on the front line.

Initially the design agency were resistant to really working closely with the developers. The first few weeks were bumpy to say the least. What turned things around was that the devs were able to bring the agency's static designs to life by building prototypes which were real web pages. To their credit, the design agency then realised (now that they could see it) the value that collaborating closely with the development team could bring.

The designers were now getting much better feedback on their designs, because the web page prototypes were much closer to a living breathing product than their static *Photoshop* files. This allowed them to iterate more quickly, which in turn led to closer and closer collaboration with the developers and the *Product Owner*. A positive feedback loop in action if ever there was one, and, importantly, one powered by customer focus: the web prototypes allowed us to get valuable feedback from customers in usability testing sessions. Our work had the feel of a start-up within a large company. And a genuinely cross-functional team.

The benefits of this approach became clear with our first release: a beautiful, simple intelligent new homepage, a full three months ahead of schedule. Our biggest hurdle in getting there was that a group of well-meaning but misguided project managers had wanted to enforce a project plan with every week planned in detail for the next three months plus.

Fortunately, I was able to persuade the transformation sponsor (the *Digital Director*) to embrace a *Minimum Viable Product (MVP)* approach instead: stakeholders and the cross-functional team mapped out collaboratively what the minimum was that we could launch with which would still give customers a great experience, hopefully. I say hopefully because even with all the right things like usability testing, it's only after launching that we could validate what we'd built with customer-based metrics. To that end we soft-launched with an A/B test which initially went to 1% of customers only, and gradually ramped up as the customer metrics improved our confidence.

If we'd gone with the project managers' desired approach there would have been the illusion of certainty, but it would have been just that: an illusion. And we'd never have able to launch three months early, as the project would have been mapped out right up until the (distant) target date.

At this point you may be thinking this is all very well but it's just one team - where's the scale? And you'd be right. By starting small, though, we were now in a great position to scale: we had a brand-new business-value-driven culture with very strong roots in that one new team. We scaled it up by adding people to our new culture progressively, not by rolling it out to lots of existing teams en masse.

Our first step in scaling up turned out to be merging in all the people from one of the pre-transformation teams. This more than doubled the number of the people in the transformation in one go. I would not recommend doing this. Adding so many people was very risky, especially as the team we were merging in had a very strong existing identity and culture, quite different to our new transformation culture.

Initially the new joiners were very reluctant to embrace a new way of working as they were very proud of and attached to their existing method: a rigid interpretation of *Scrum*. The worst thing we could have done at this point would have been to impose our new way of working on them. Imposing change is one of the big traps which many transformations fall into – it never works, as the people receiving the imposition reject the change.

Instead, we said: "We appreciate that you come from separate teams with historically different ways of working, and that we're now asking you to work together. We know it's a big ask. We'd like you to evolve a new way of working together, and it's up to you to evolve it. Take what's worked well for you before, and let's evolve from there."

Empowering the people doing the work to evolve their way of working together had many positive effects. The barriers came down and the new joiners opened their minds to new ways of doing things. They relished the sense of purpose that came with being given customer-focused goals to work on rather than pre-defined solutions. And they loved collaborating closely with their *Product Owner* every day, rather than just once per sprint.

Our way of working continued to evolve; the melting pot of the new joiners and the original team forged lots of new ideas.

Some ideas worked very well and some didn't; we kept the ones which did and discarded the rest. We were reaping the rewards of responding to change over following a plan, through a culture of experimentation.

As Dan Pink revealed in his excellent book *Drive1*, people crave autonomy, mastery and purpose in their working lives. By giving the developers the freedom to focus on solving problems for customers, we gave them autonomy and purpose. Mastery came along too – the work now provided intrinsic motivation for the developers, and consequently the quality of their work went through the roof. Your developers are very often better than you think – rather than trying to upskill them, often all you need to do is give them interesting challenges to solve.

So, it was our focus on customer value which allowed us to cope with more than doubling in size in one go. By this I mean allowing everyone to focus on customer value, including the people who actually do the work. The great thing about all this is that focusing on customer value is also the right thing to do for your customers, of course! The business stakeholders continued to be delighted with the quality of the work. That's the main takeaway: customer focus is the vehicle to allow cultural transformation while delivering on business goals at the same time. It's not a case of trying to shoehorn them together as a cost-cutting measure, it's the right thing to do because the sharp focus on business goals allows the cultural transformation to happen.

Further evidence of this came when the next part of the scaling challenge arrived: we now had to merge in a brand-new group of 30-40 people, most of whom were new hires, in a remote location. How could we retain our carefully grown culture and the autonomy we wanted our teams to have, while also ensuring alignment between them?

We did so by making customer focus the key ingredient of our teams. Instead of fitting the work around our teams, we spun up small autonomous teams on demand around particular customer-facing goals. This gave us some significant benefits. Flexibility: we could ensure that each team comprised people with the right combination of skills to deliver its business goal. Delivery of value: because each team had a clear business goal, it was focused on delivering value. If we'd tried to make the work fit around pre-defined teams then these business goals would have been diluted.

The challenge with our model was how to ensure cohesion and harmony between team members, particularly if people were going to be working with different people every few months (or weeks). We leaned heavily on the *Spotify 2* model here, bringing in the concept of a tribe for a group of c.50-100 people, aligned around a high-level business goal. Perfect for scaling. The tribe had a name, a mission statement, and tribe-level rituals such as planning and retrospectives. These provided the common bonds and identity needed to provide cohesion and harmony when new teams were spun up.

Incidentally, I've since worked on a transformation in another organisation which also brought in the concept of tribes. They didn't construct the tribes around business value, however, and the result was an ineffective shuffling of the deck without any tangible transformation at all. So, the message isn't that the *Spotify* model (or any other methodology) is a silver bullet, it's that your transformation will fail if you don't underpin it with a laser focus on customer value.

To maximise harmony, we also minimised the number of roles in our teams. Essentially we boiled it down to developers and *Product Owners*, with other roles floating outside the teams and being pulled in on demand. This minimised hand-offs and therefore friction and silos – all of which damage customer focus when present.

It might not be palatable to some in your organisation, but if you don't minimise the number of roles then you're greatly restricting your ability to transform.

Another takeaway is that successful transformations require senior leadership to be on board, and strategic product management to be in place. Without either of these things you will fail, no matter how long you spend trying to make your teams more agile.

To sum up: if your goal is an agile transformation, the best way to achieve it is through customer focus. Don't treat the two as separate entities - roll them together by empowering the people who do the work to come up with the solutions.

References

- Pink. D. (2009). *Drive: The Surprising Truth About What Motivates Us*. Riverhead Books.

- https://labs.spotify.com/2014/03/27/spotify-engineering-culture-part-1/

About John Boyes

John is an agile coach who is passionate about helping teams deliver value through focusing on the customer.

He's an independent thinker who loves to help organisations find their innovation mojo by empowering the people who do the work. John has been working with agile teams since 2005 and has rich and varied experience as a coach, scrum master and developer.

He still loves writing code and finds that his in-depth technical knowledge combined with his value-driven approach really helps him to get the best out of teams and to foster great collaboration between developers and business people.

https://www.linkedin.com/in/john-boyes/

Join Agility Gigs

Agility Gigs is an initiative of London-based *Sullivan & Stanley*. It is a collective of CTO's, Product Specialists and Agility Coaches. The community networks in real time and meets to debate the future of Change, Tech, Agile, Work and other interesting topics raised in the group.

This is an independent group with no vendor pressure to support you on your journey.

For more information please visit *www.agilitygigs.com* and get in contact.

All proceeds from the sale of this book are being donated to *Cancer Central* at *www.cancercentral.org.uk/*

Lightning Source UK Ltd.
Milton Keynes UK
UKHW021439141218
333964UK00003B/94/P